Bukakkemon 2
The Second Cumming!

Alexis Hex

Welcome to the Fromunda Region.

Adventurer we need your assistance.
There as been an outbreak of infectious creatures
known as Bukakkemon.

Please head directly to the free clinic and find
Prof. Snatch.

She will give you all the information you need.

Greetings I'm Prof. Snatch. Thank you for coming.

The Bukakkemon outbreak has gotten out of control.

I need your help to put together my report for the center of disease control.

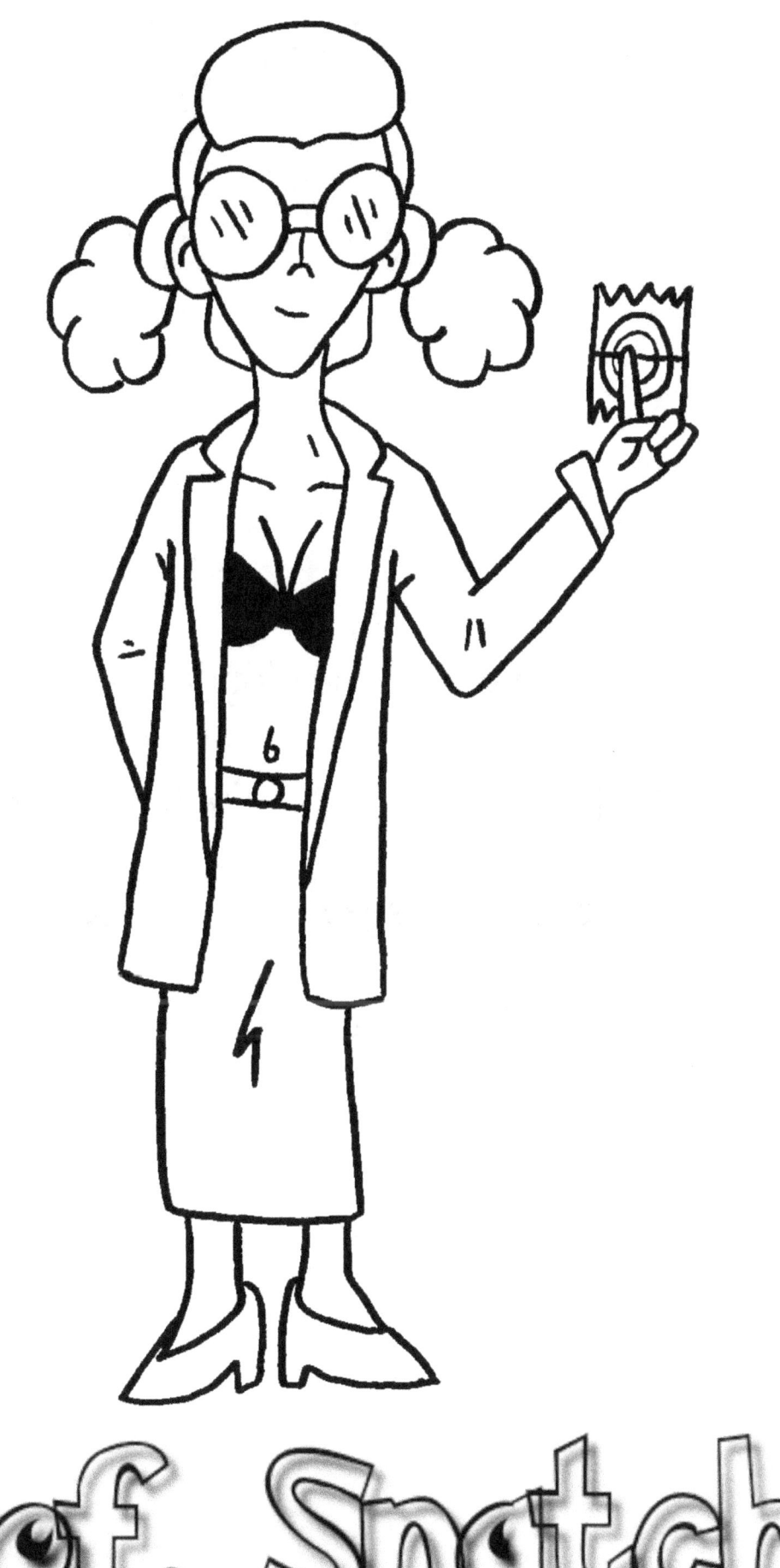

Prof. Snatch

Take some of these Condominators.

Simply rip open the wrapper to catch a Bukakkemon.

If you need more stop in at any free clinic.

Good luck!

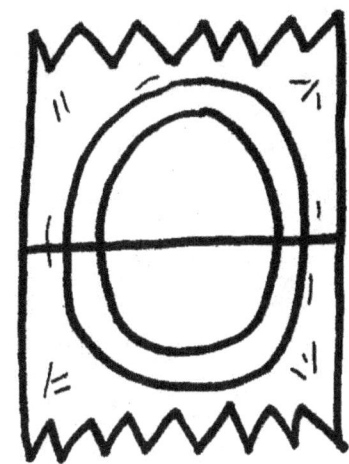

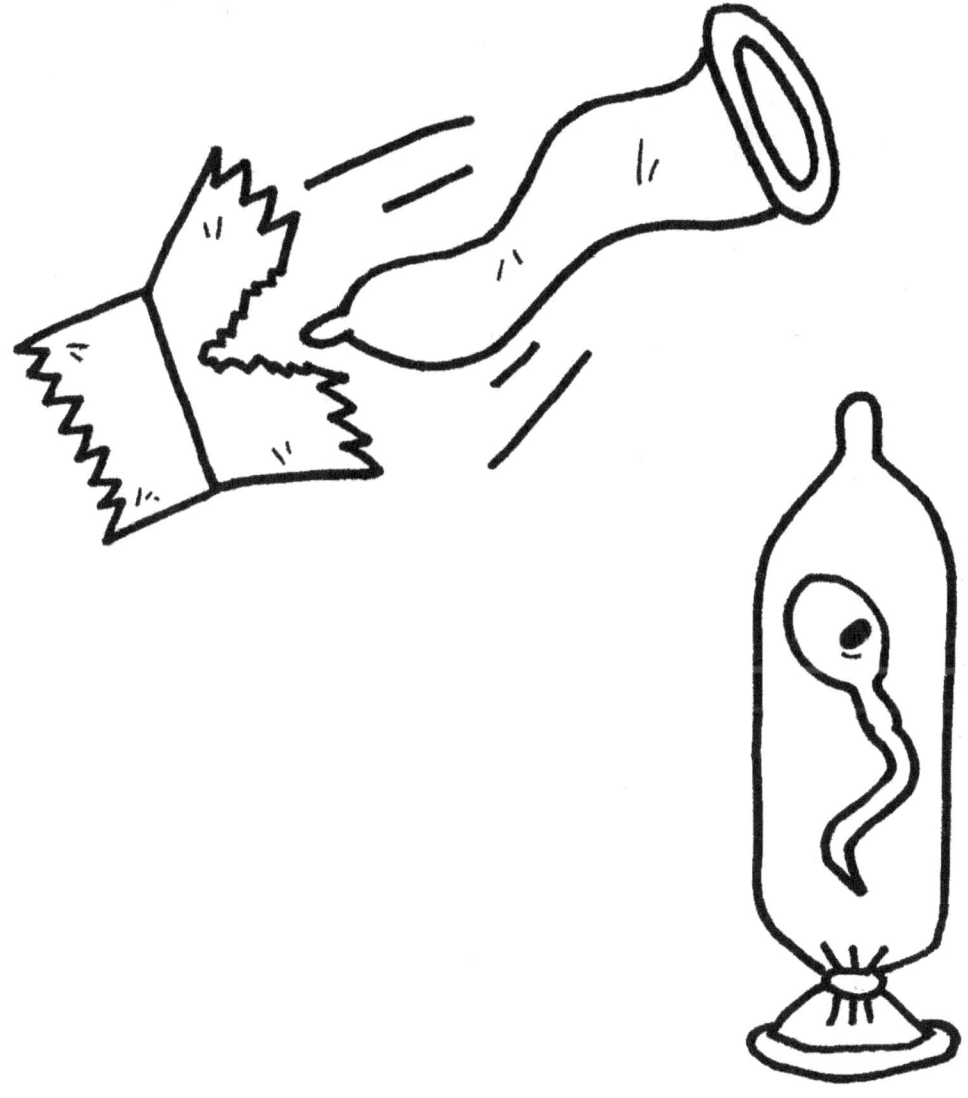

Condomintators

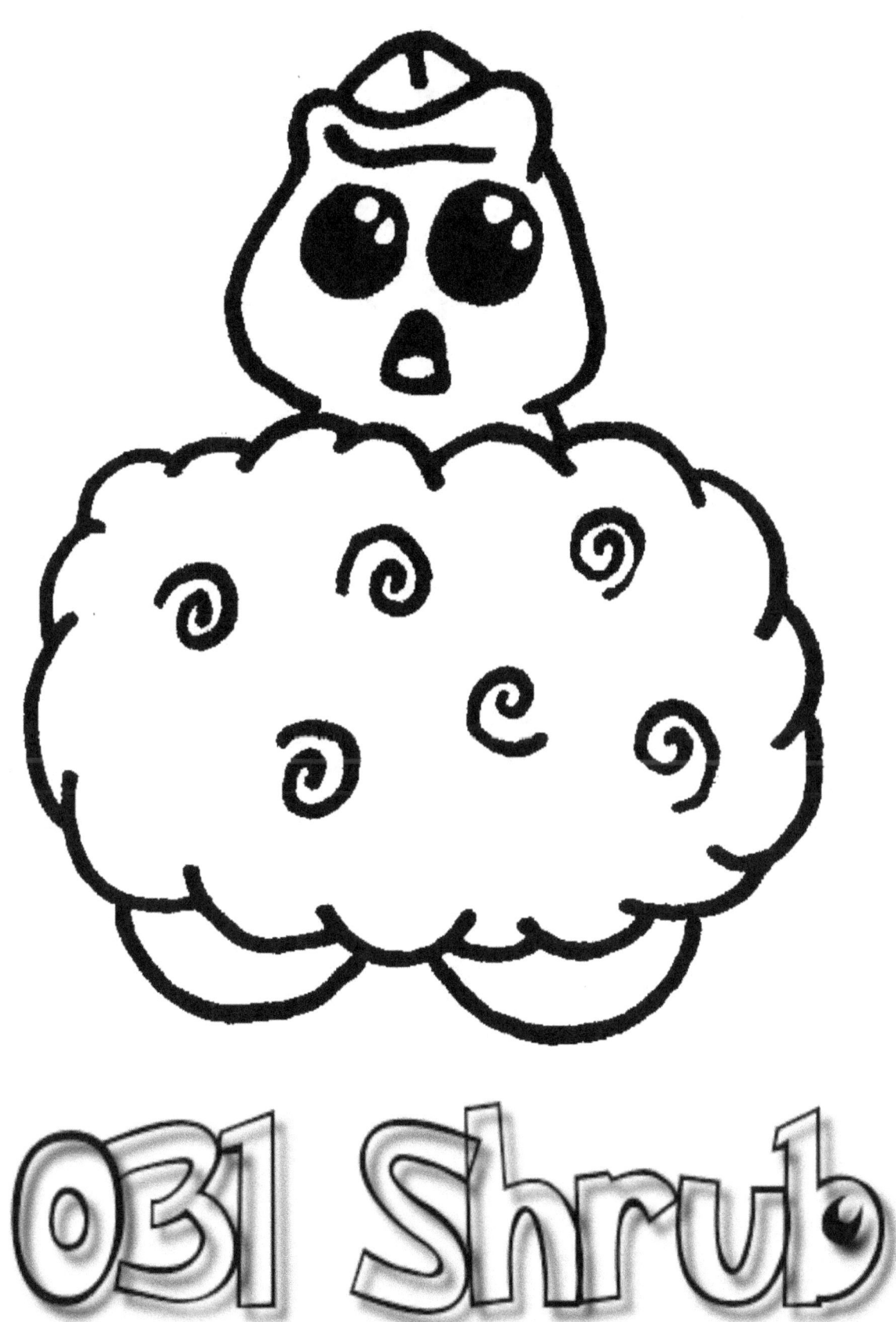

031 Shrub

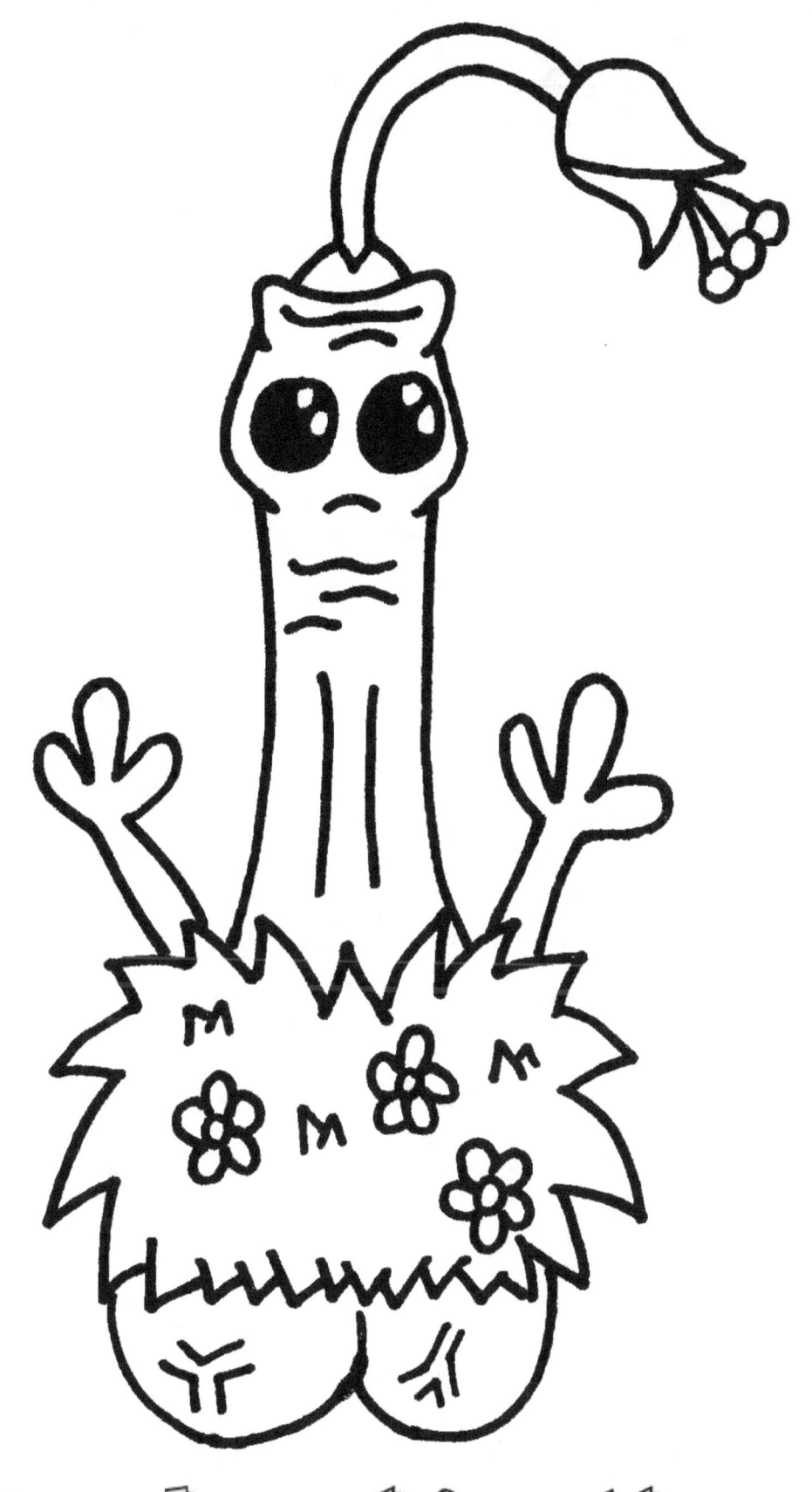

032 Whorticulture

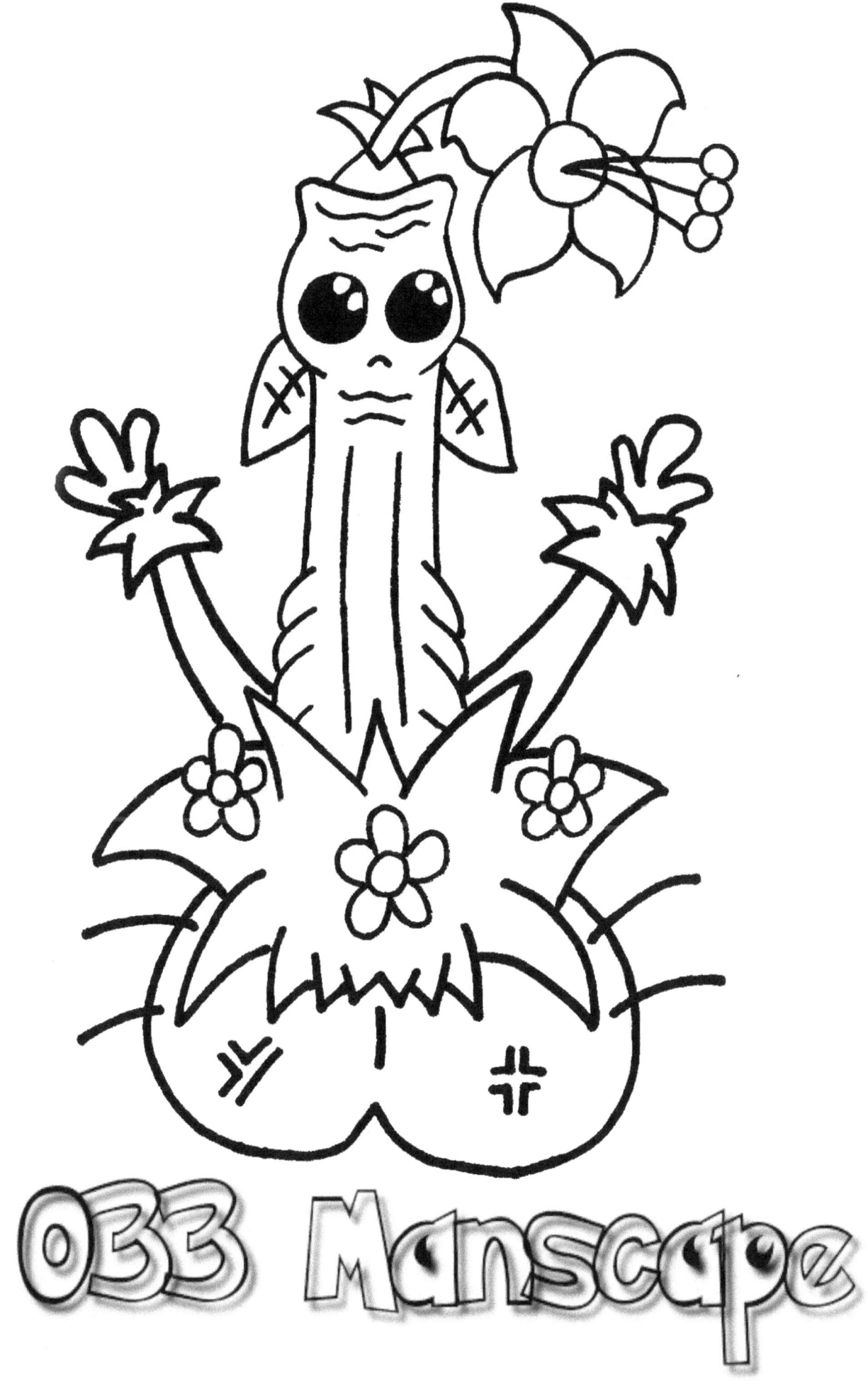

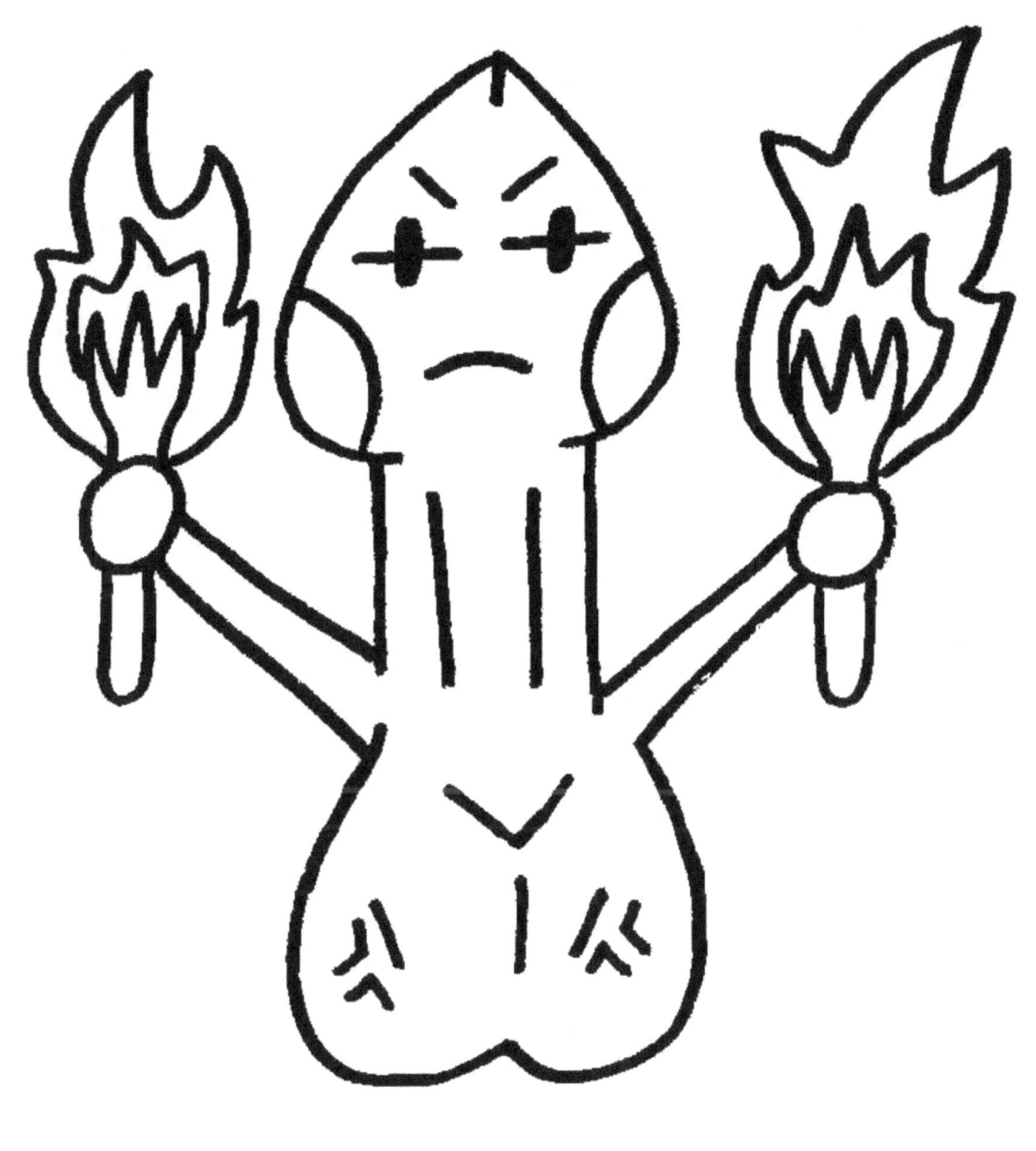

034 Hotlink

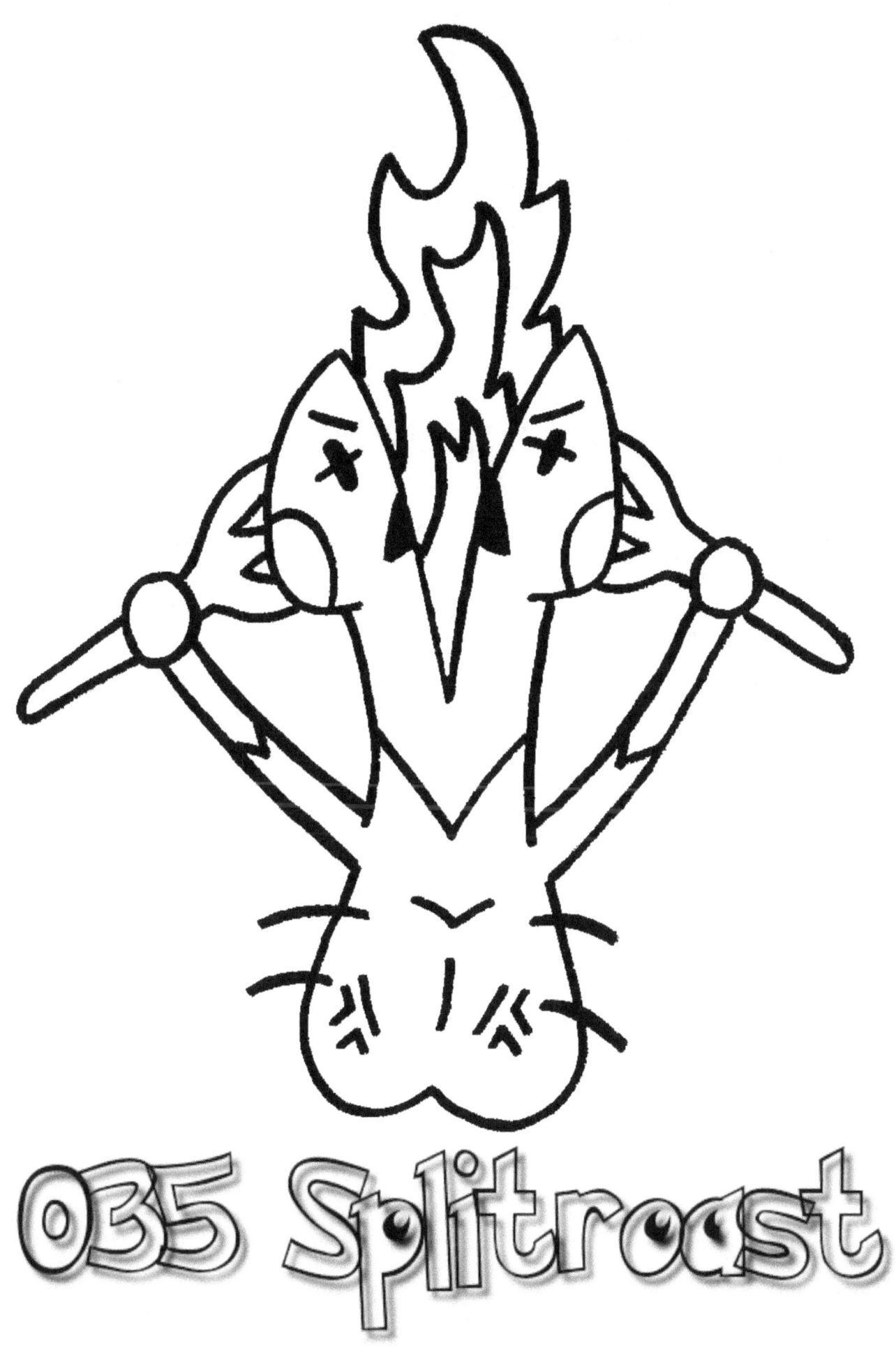

035 Splitroast

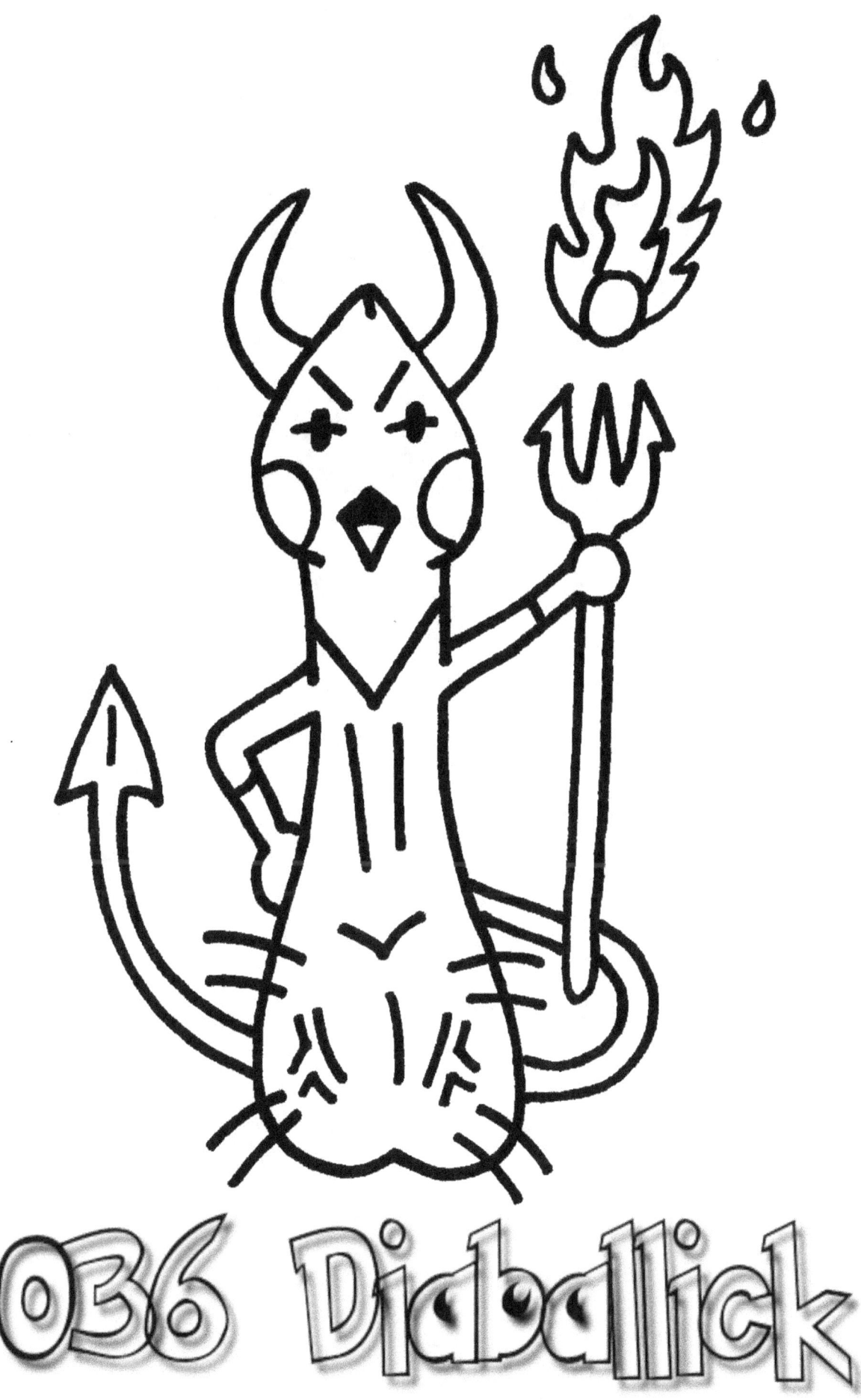

036 Diaballick

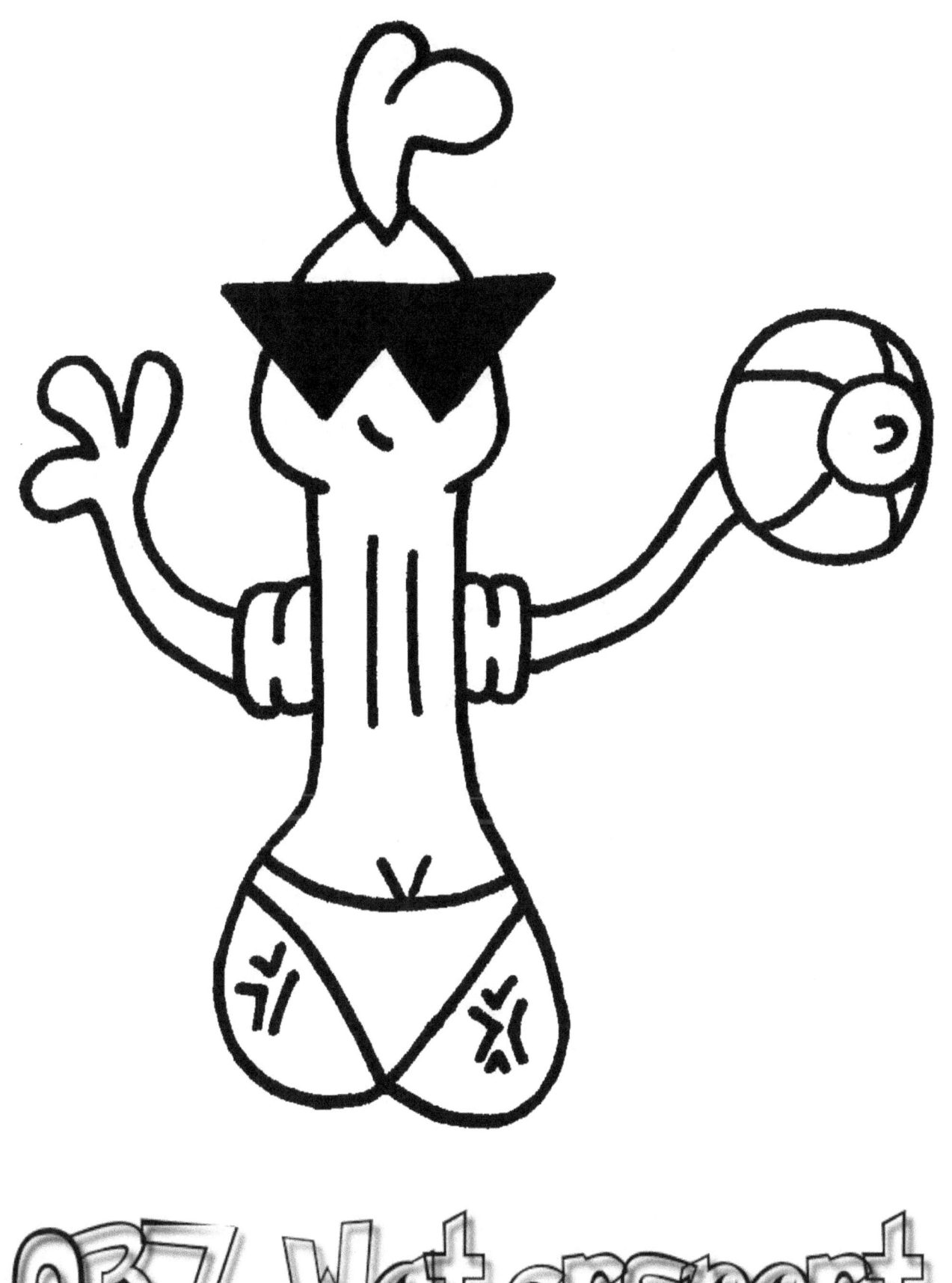

037/ Watersport

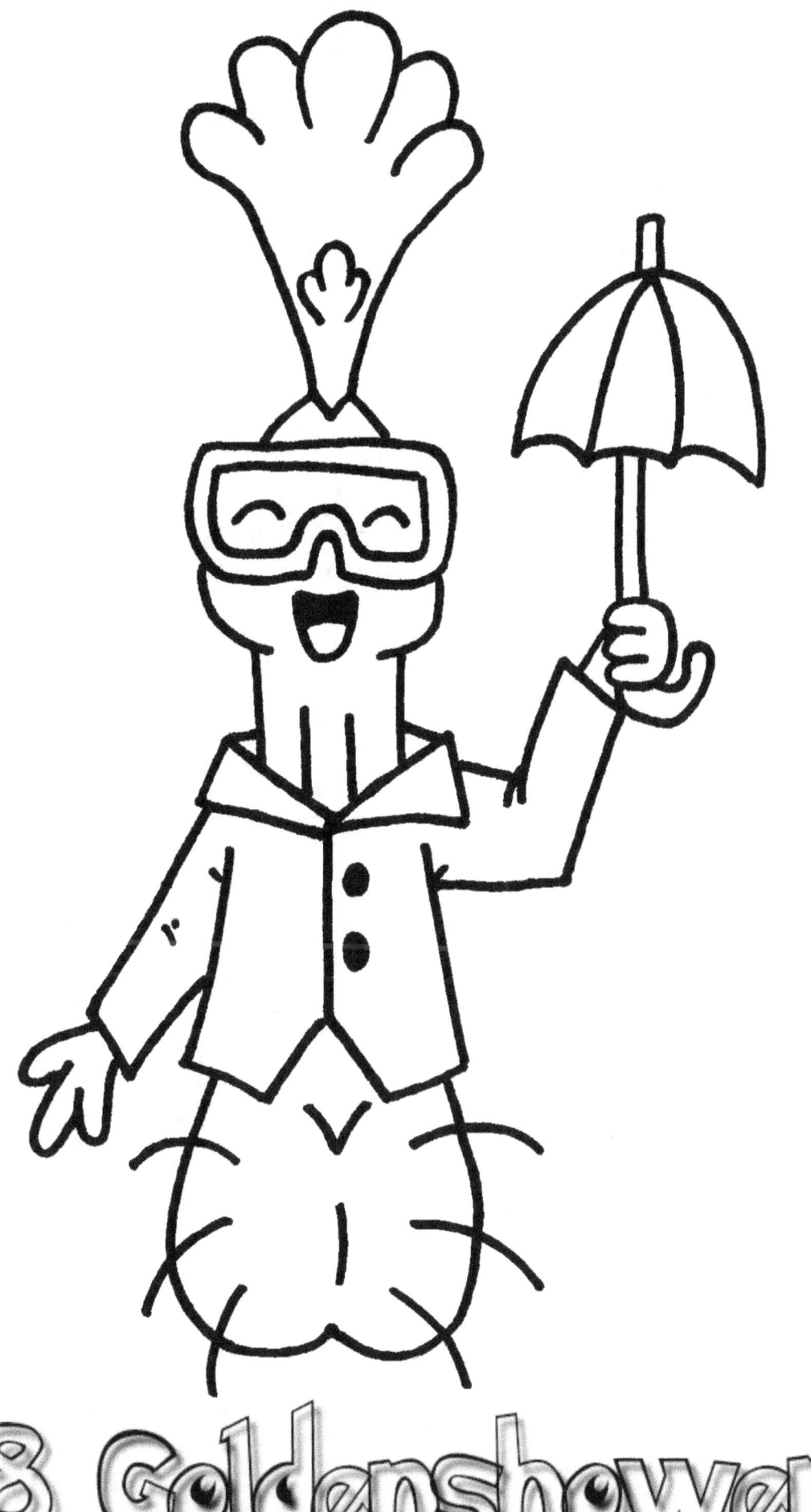

038 Goldenshower

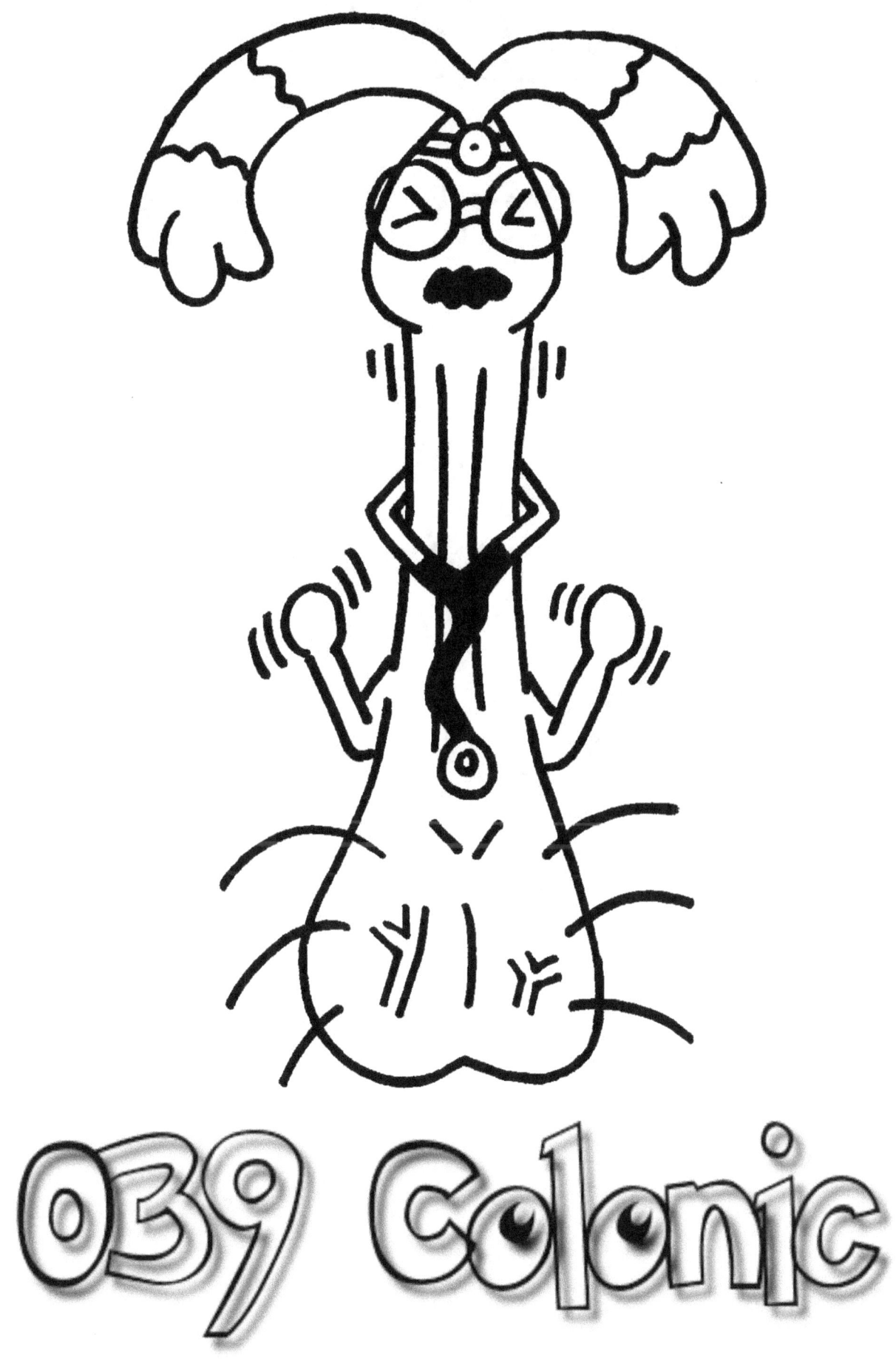

039 Colonic

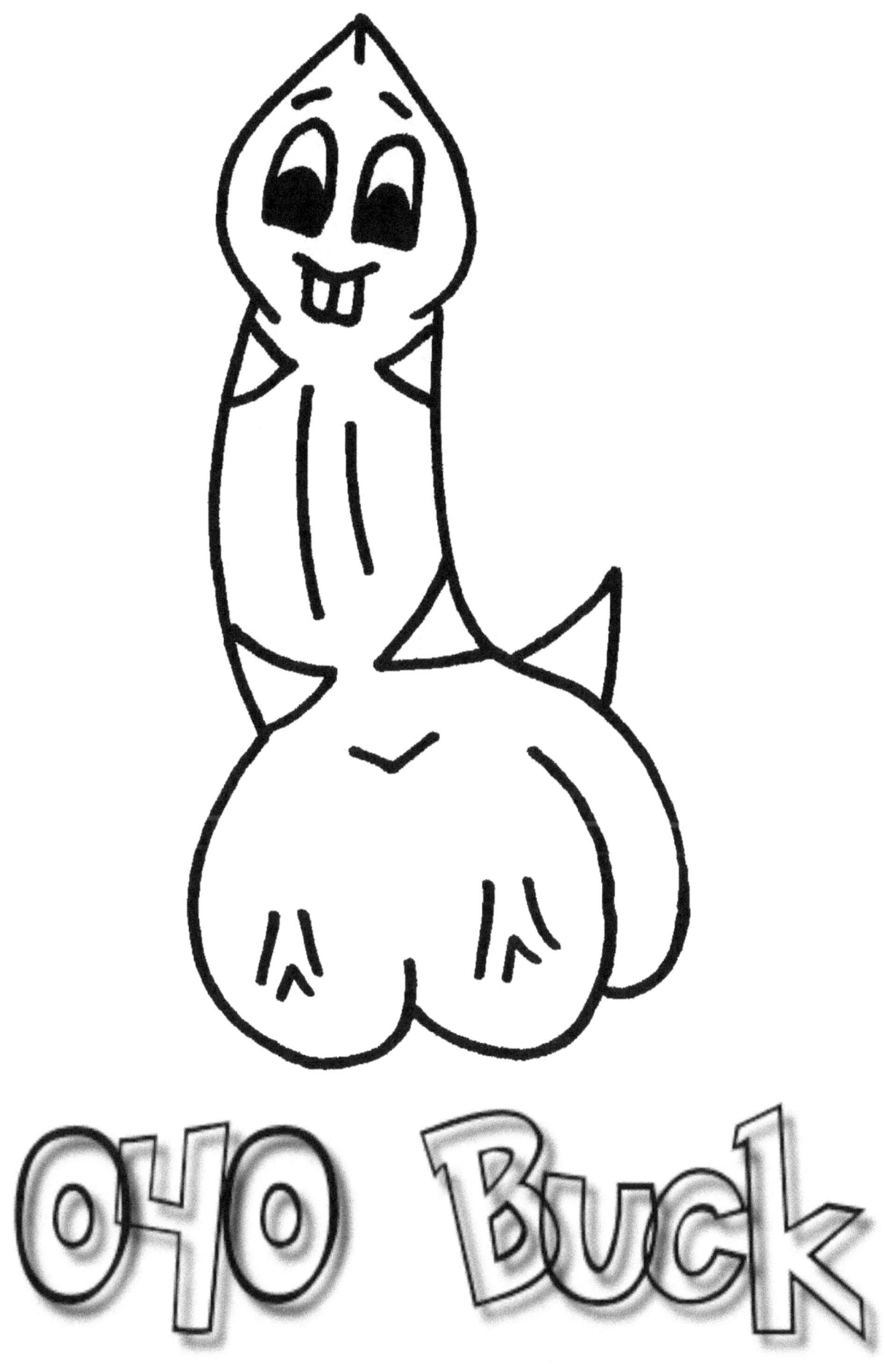

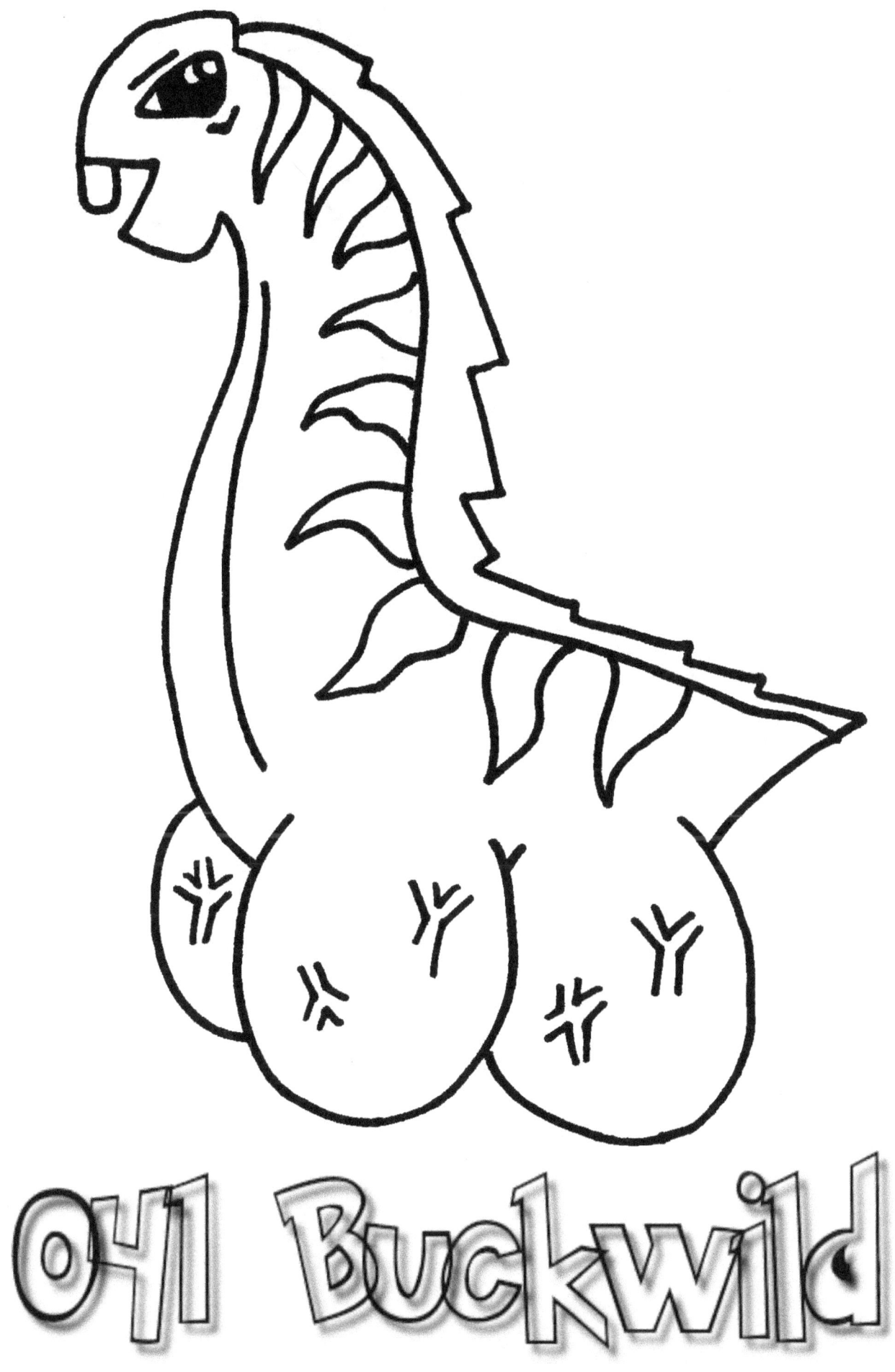

041 Buckwild

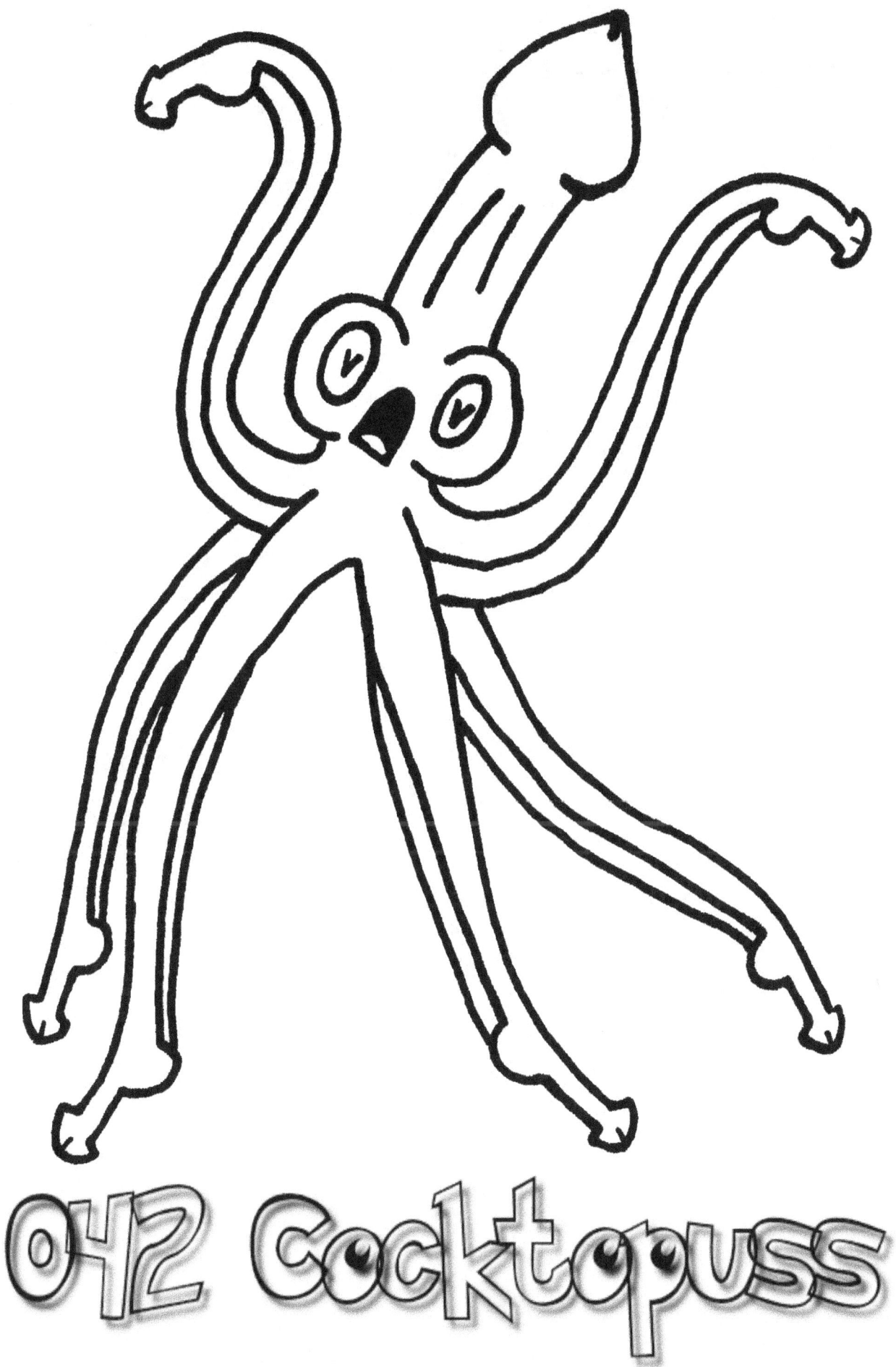

042 Cocktopuss

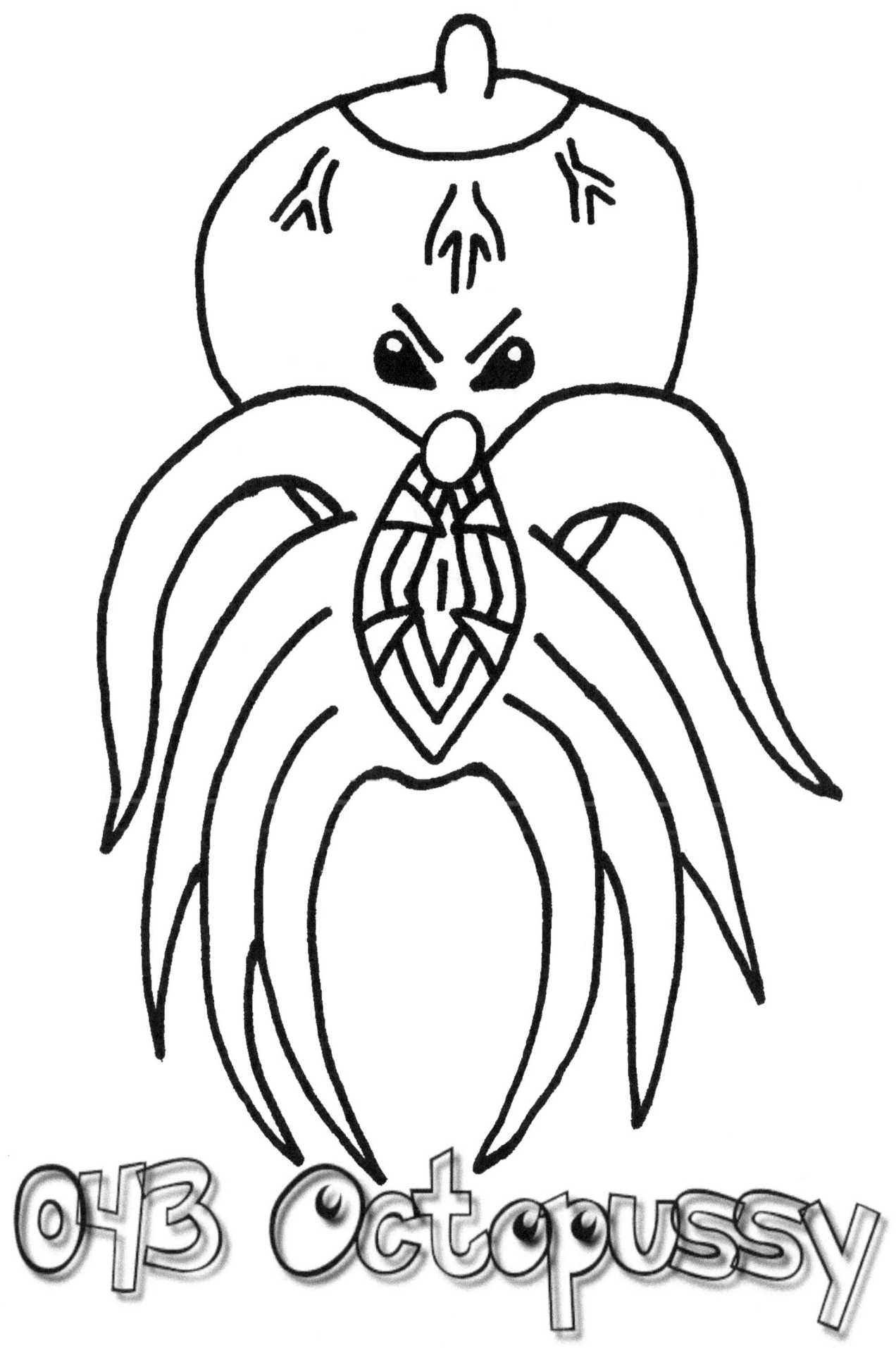

043 Octopussy

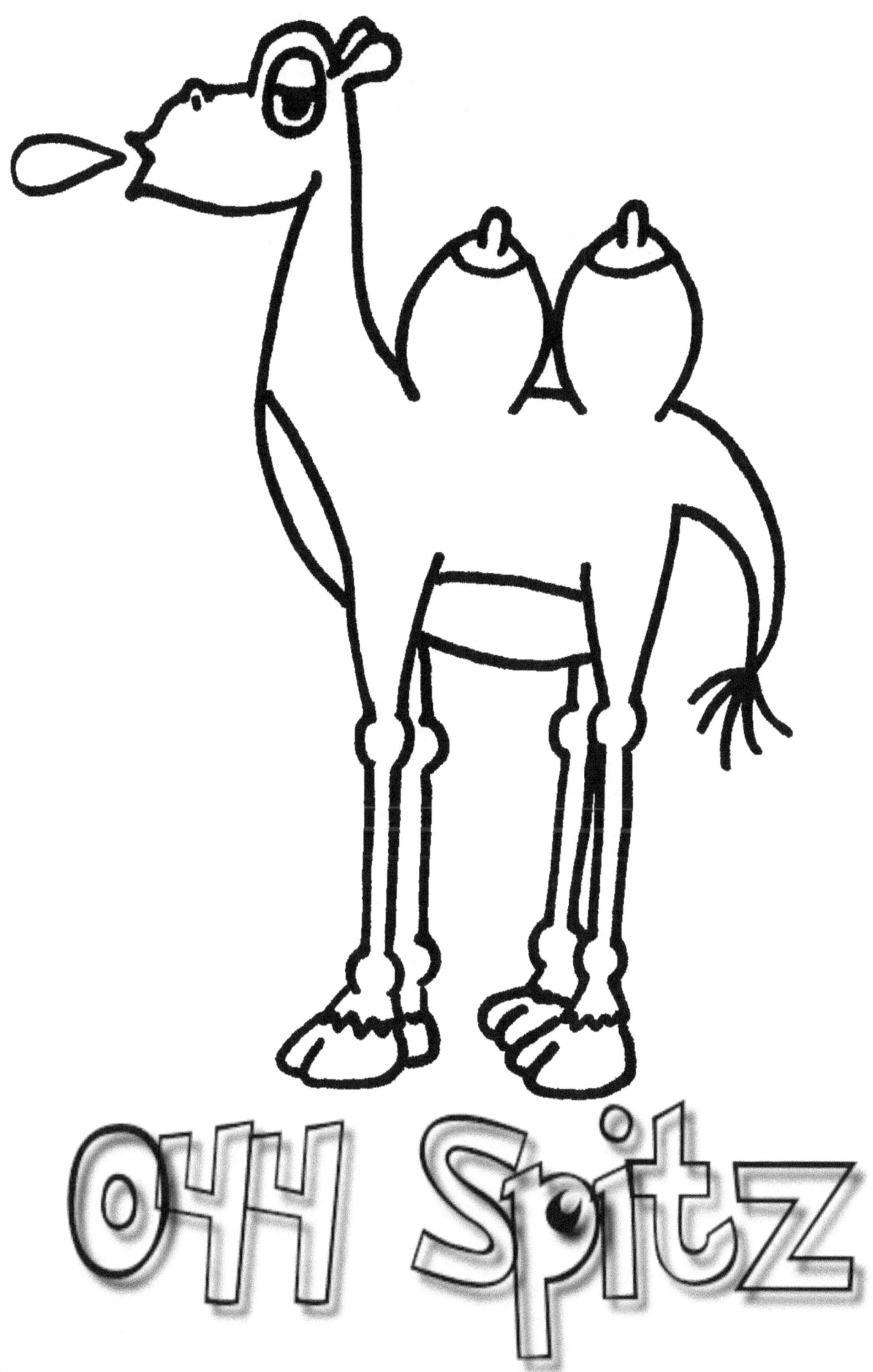

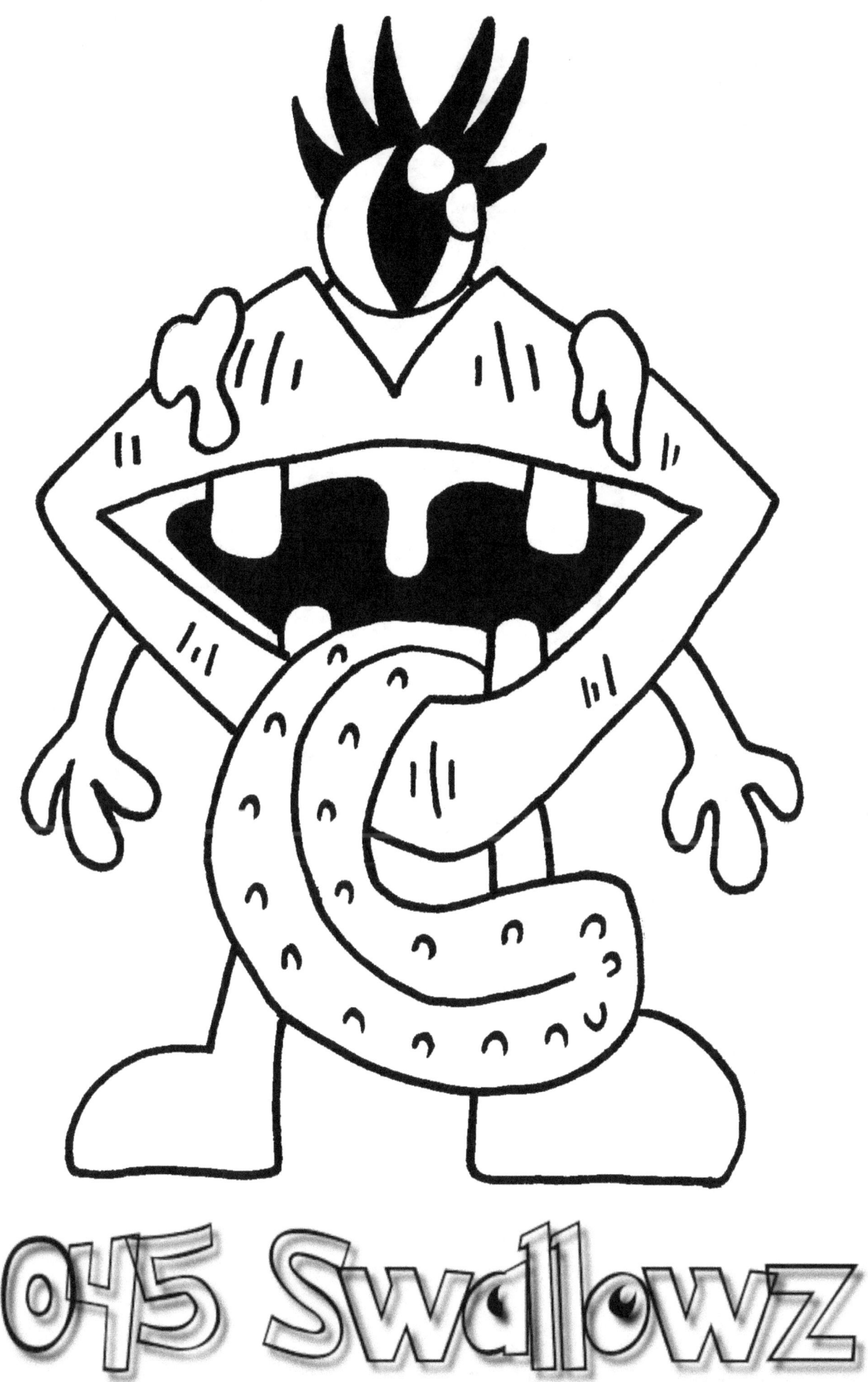

045 Swallowz

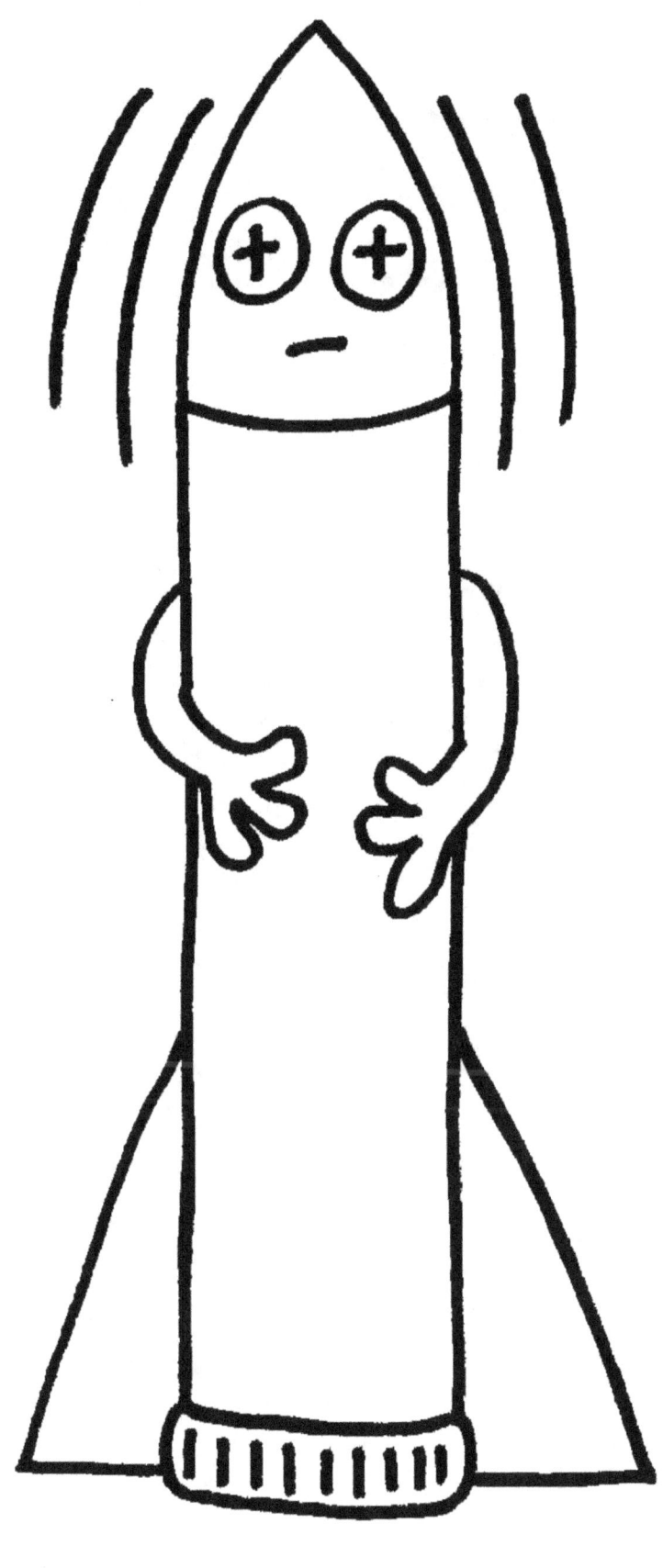

046 Pocket Rocket

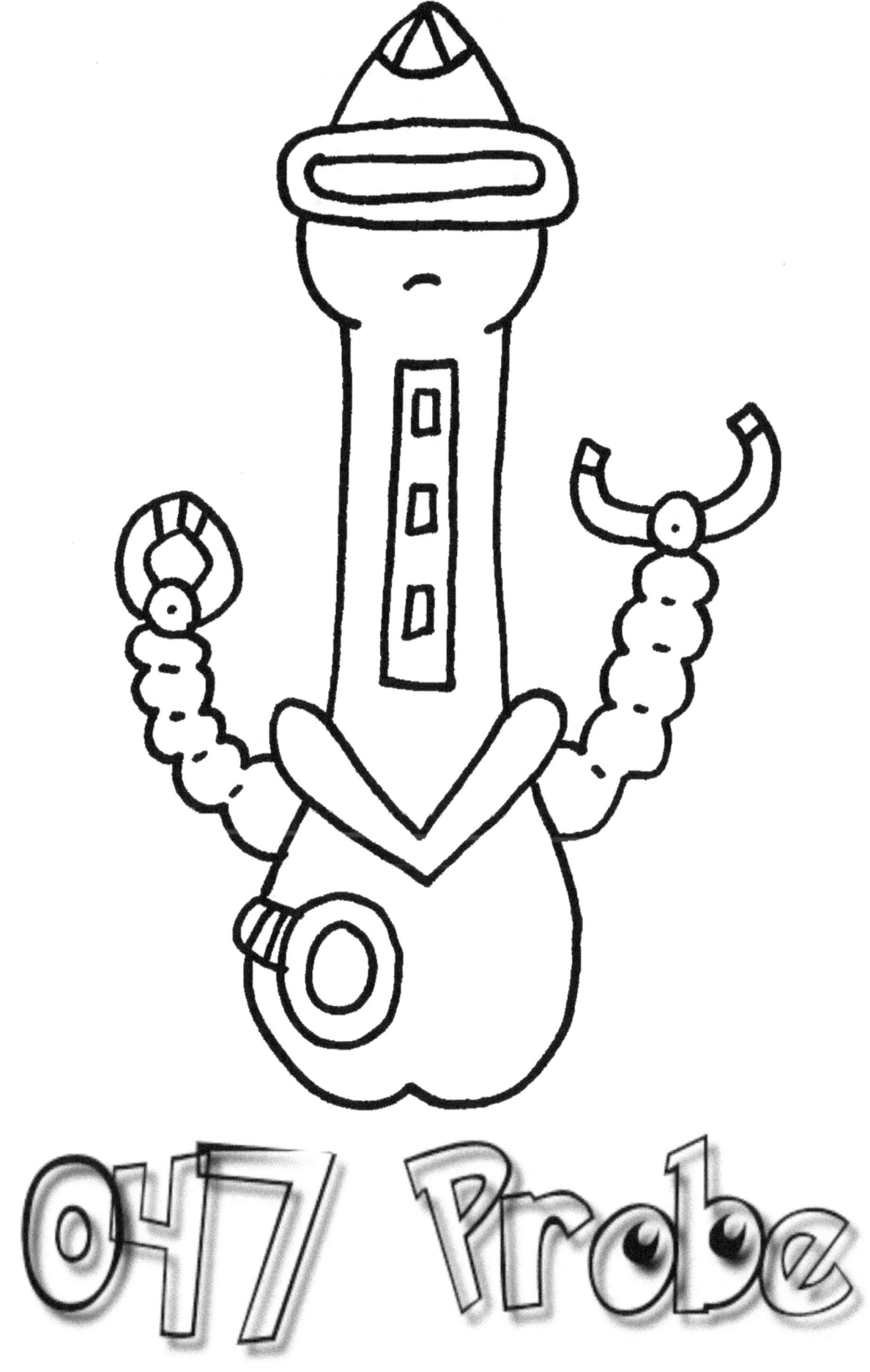

047 Probe

048 Skinflute

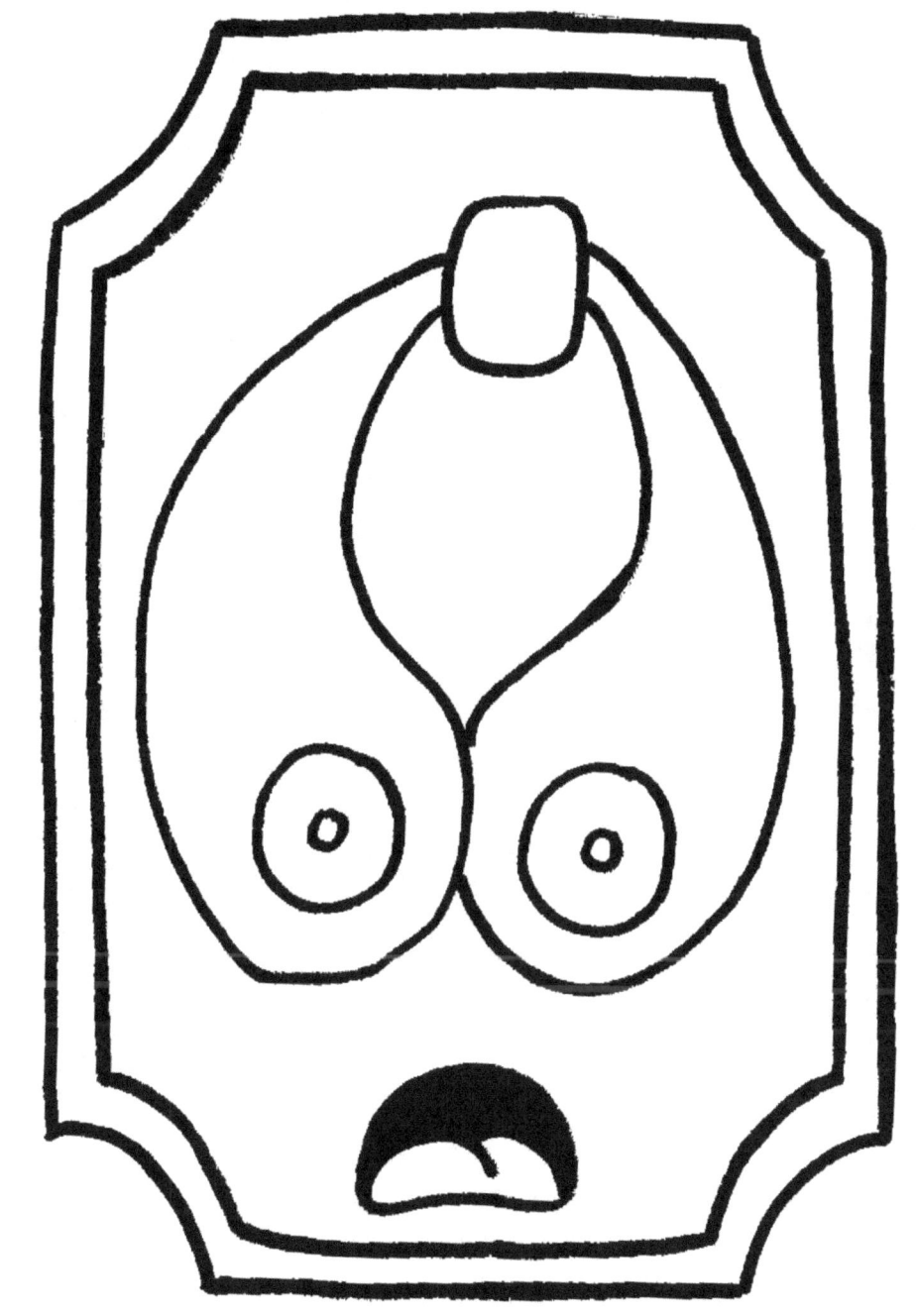

049 Knockerz

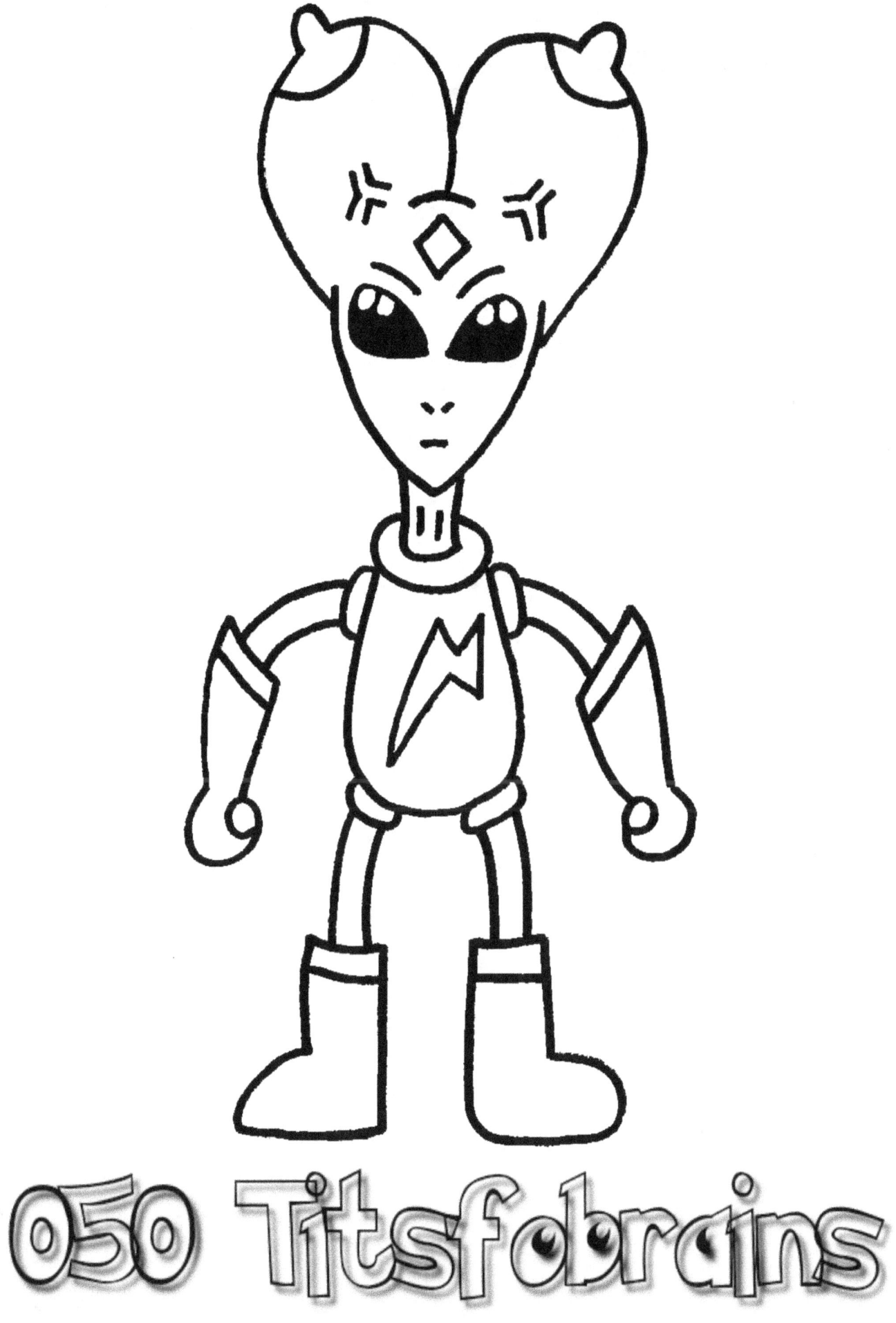

050 Titsfobrains

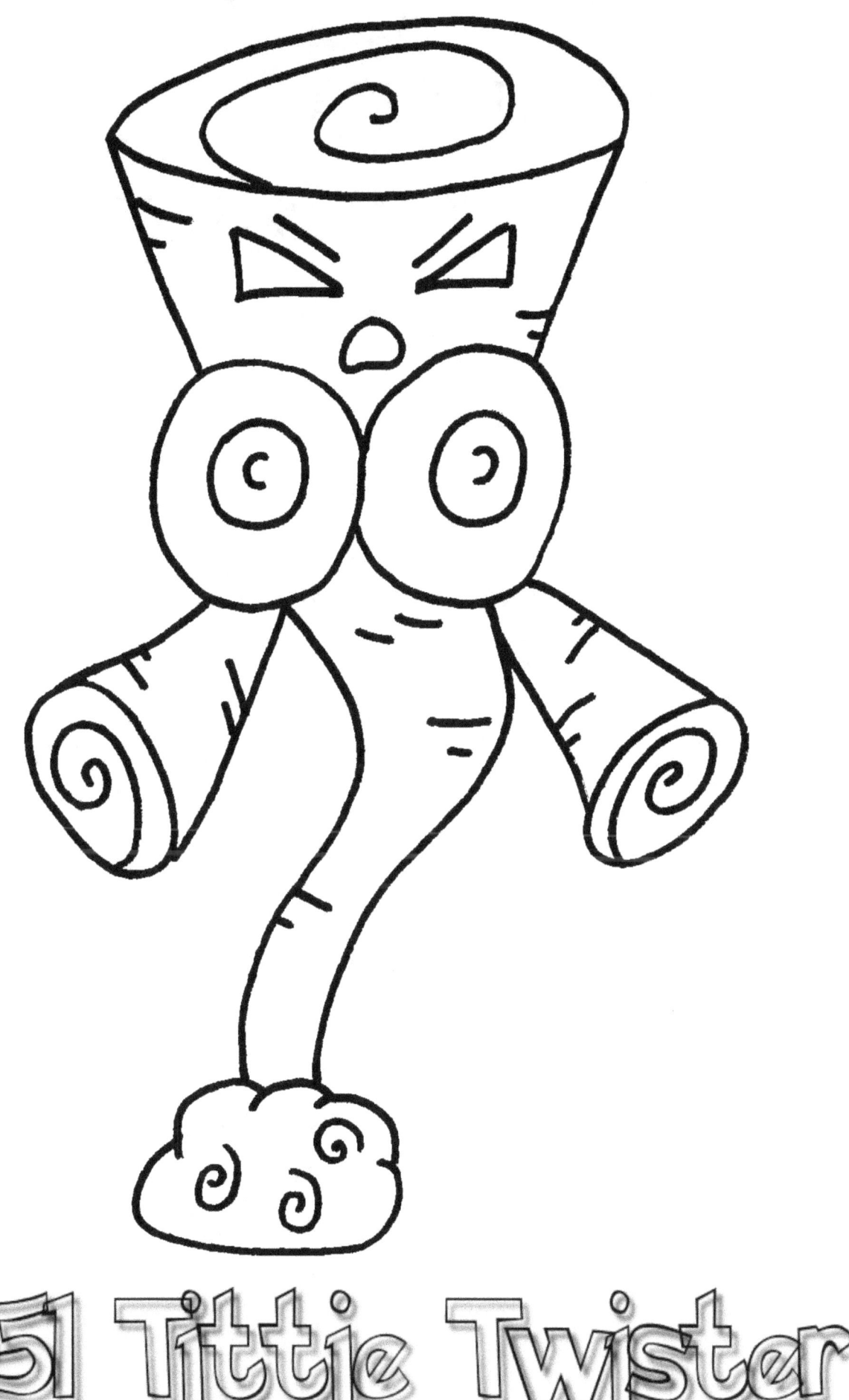

051 Tittie Twister

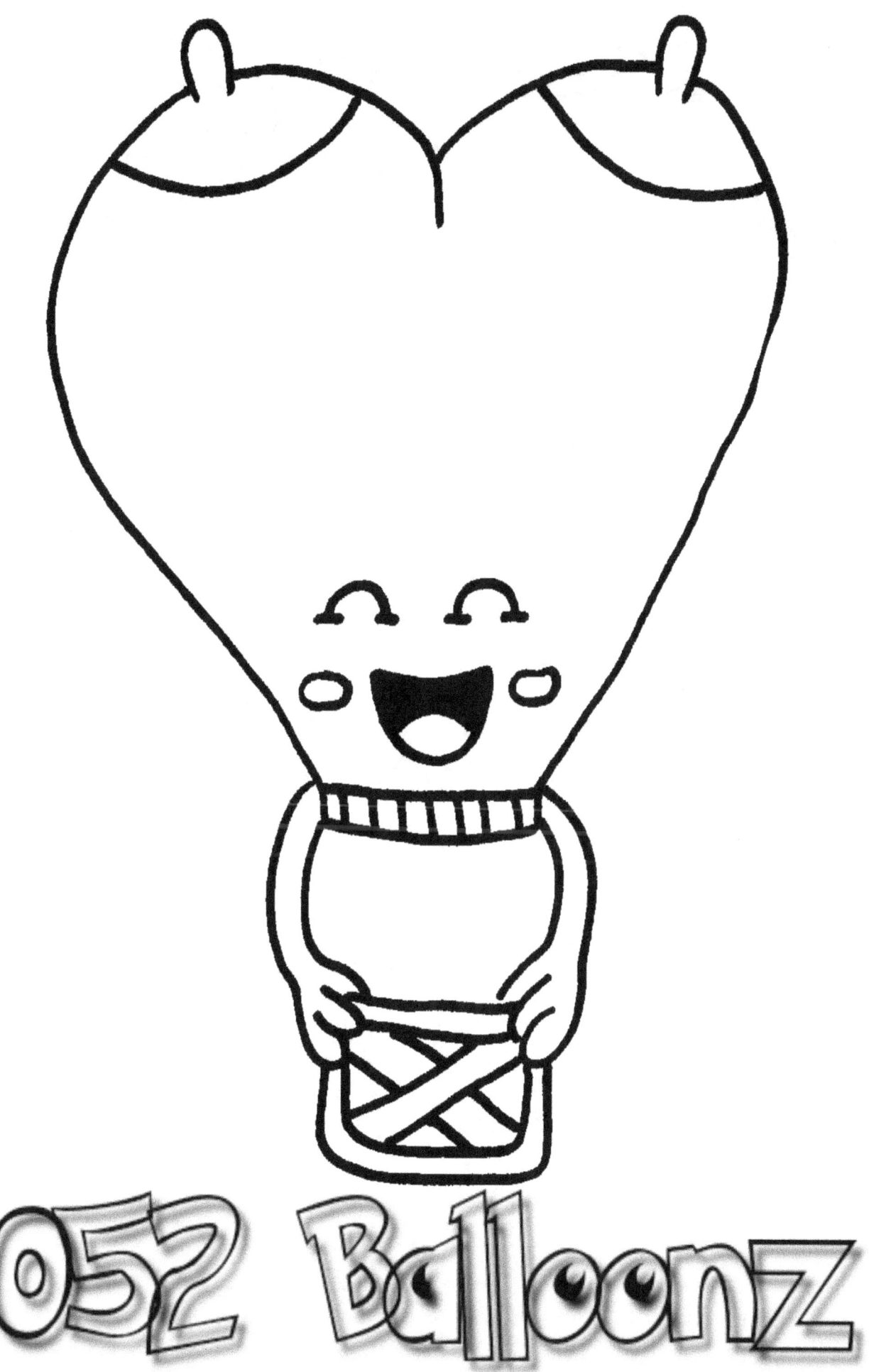

052 Balloonz

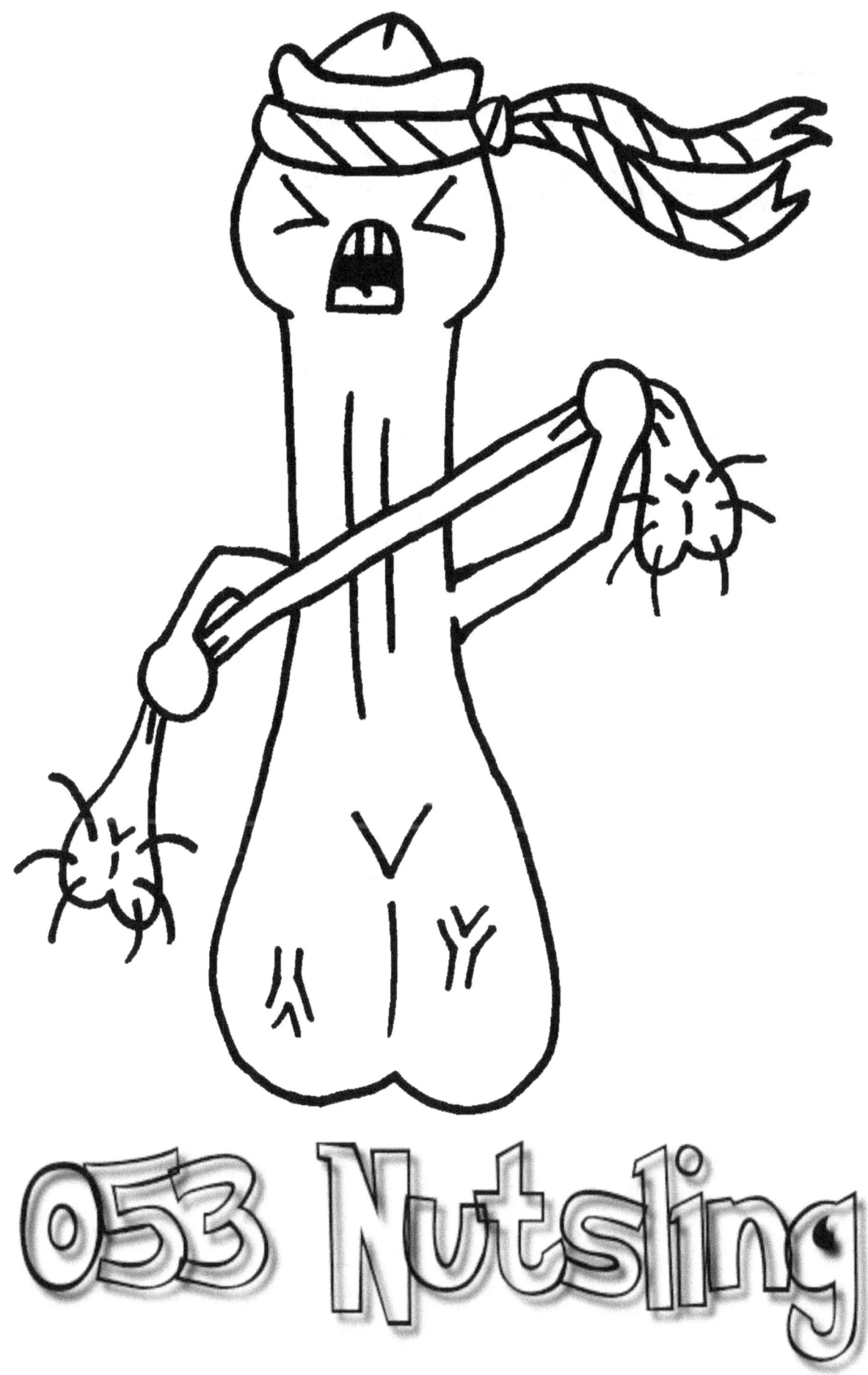

053 Nutsling

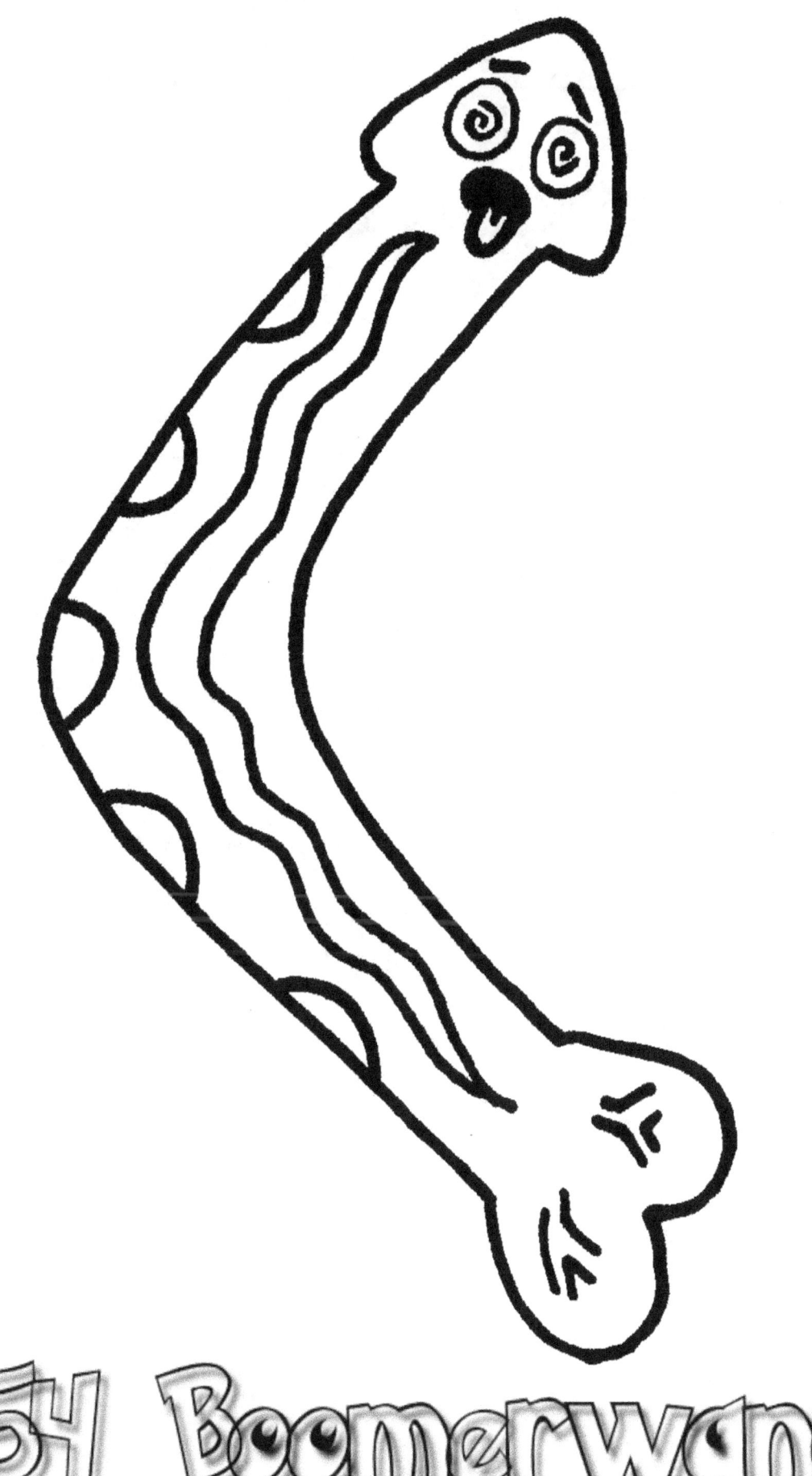

054 Boomerwang

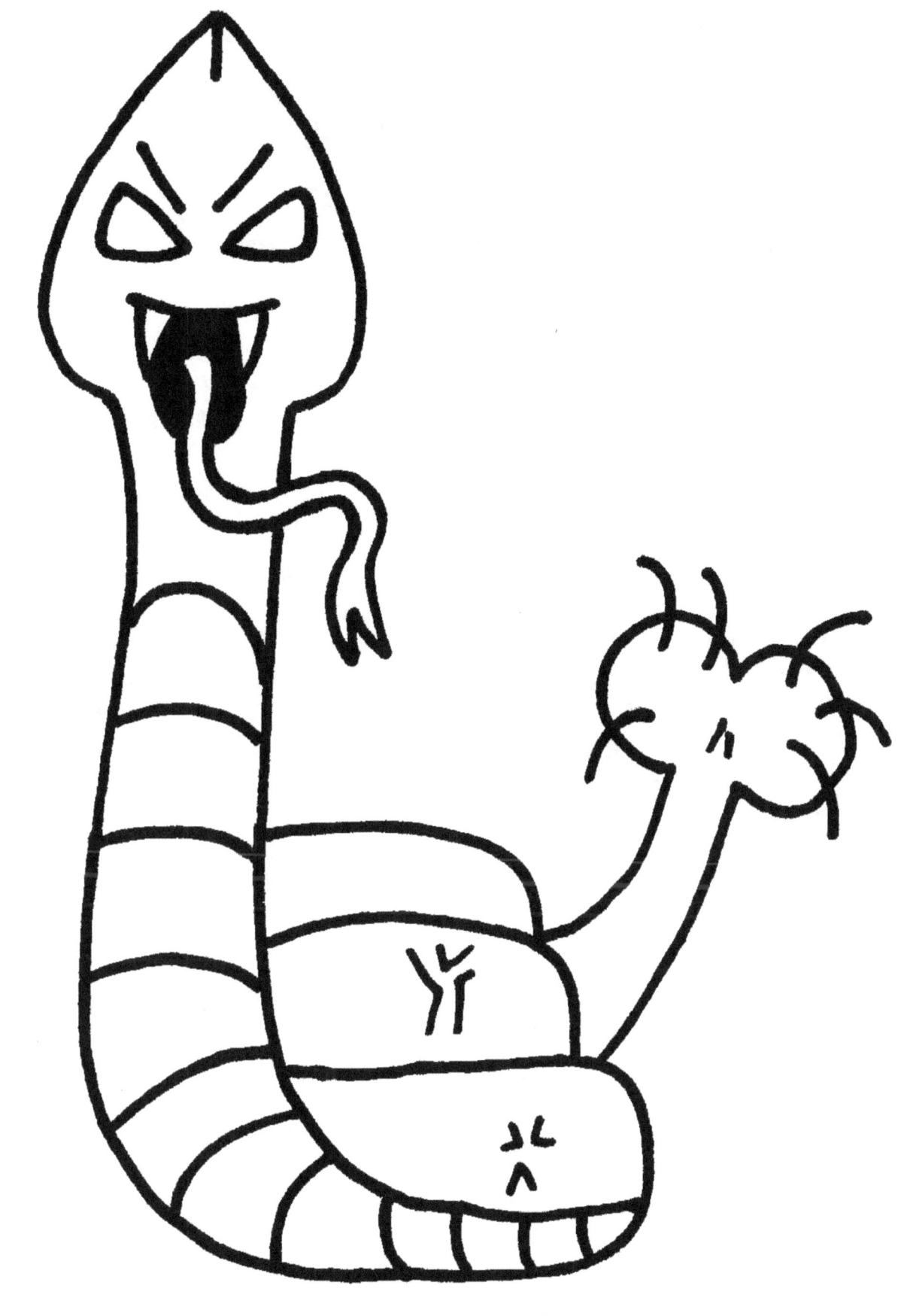

055 Trowser Snake

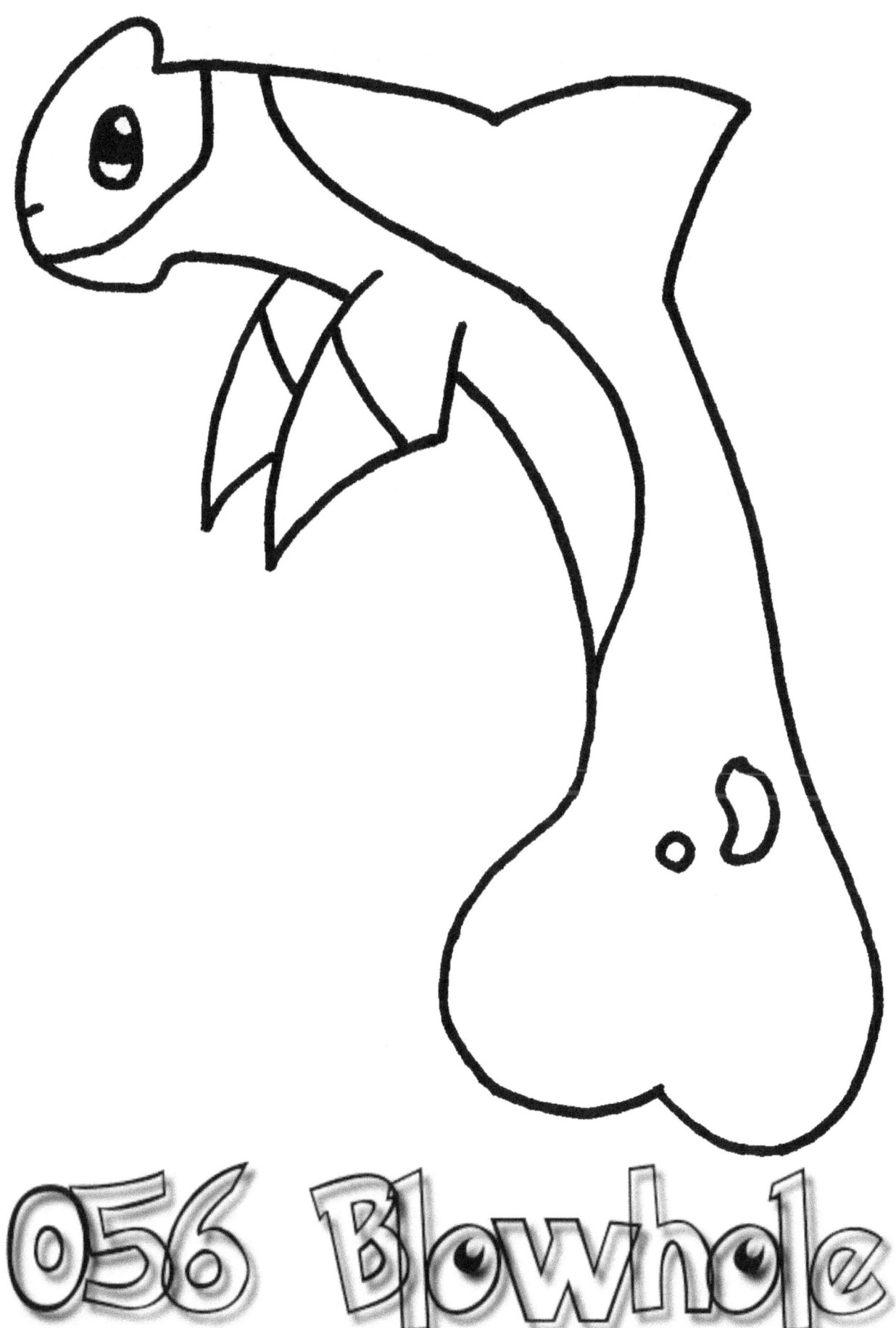

056 Blowhole

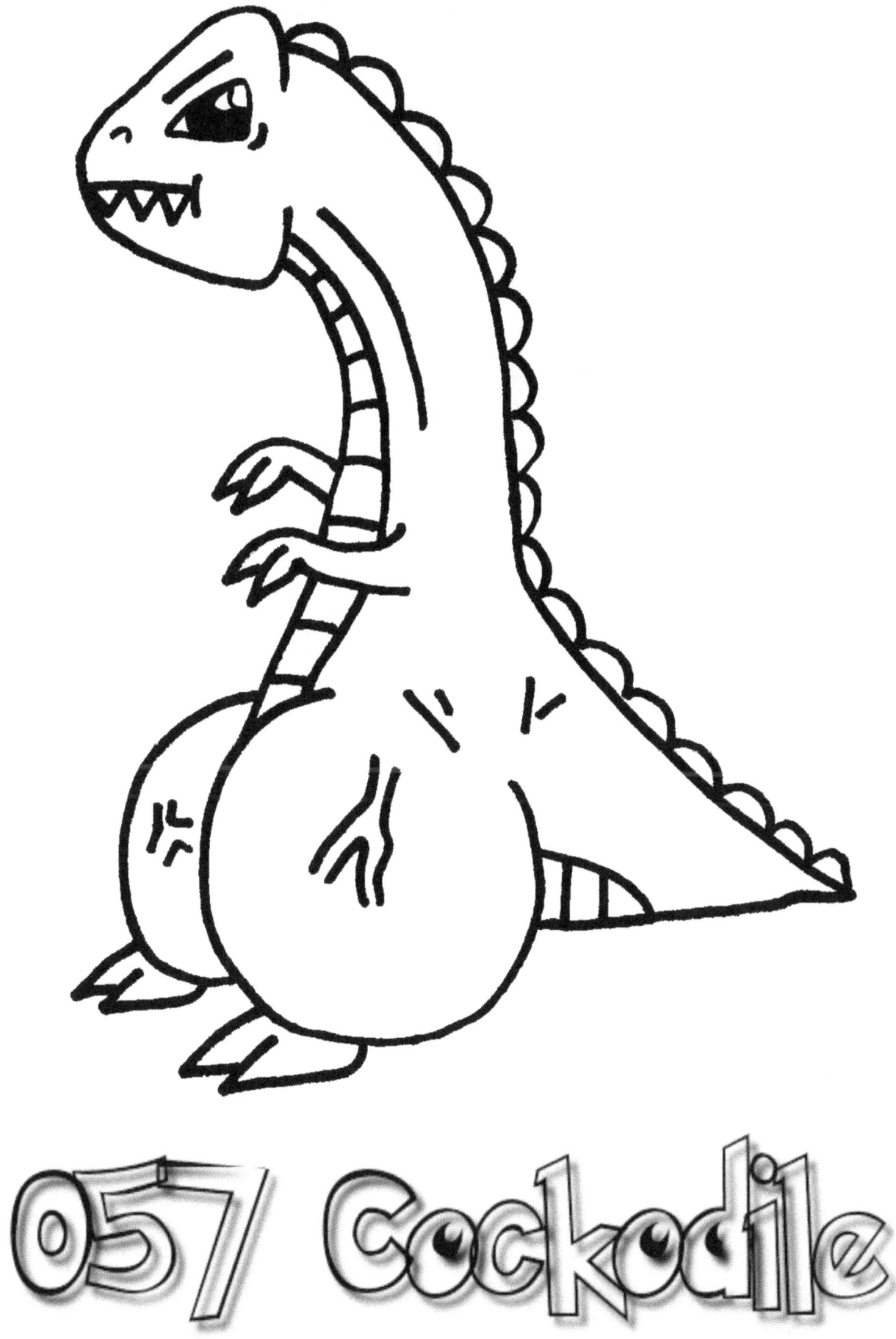

057 Cockodile

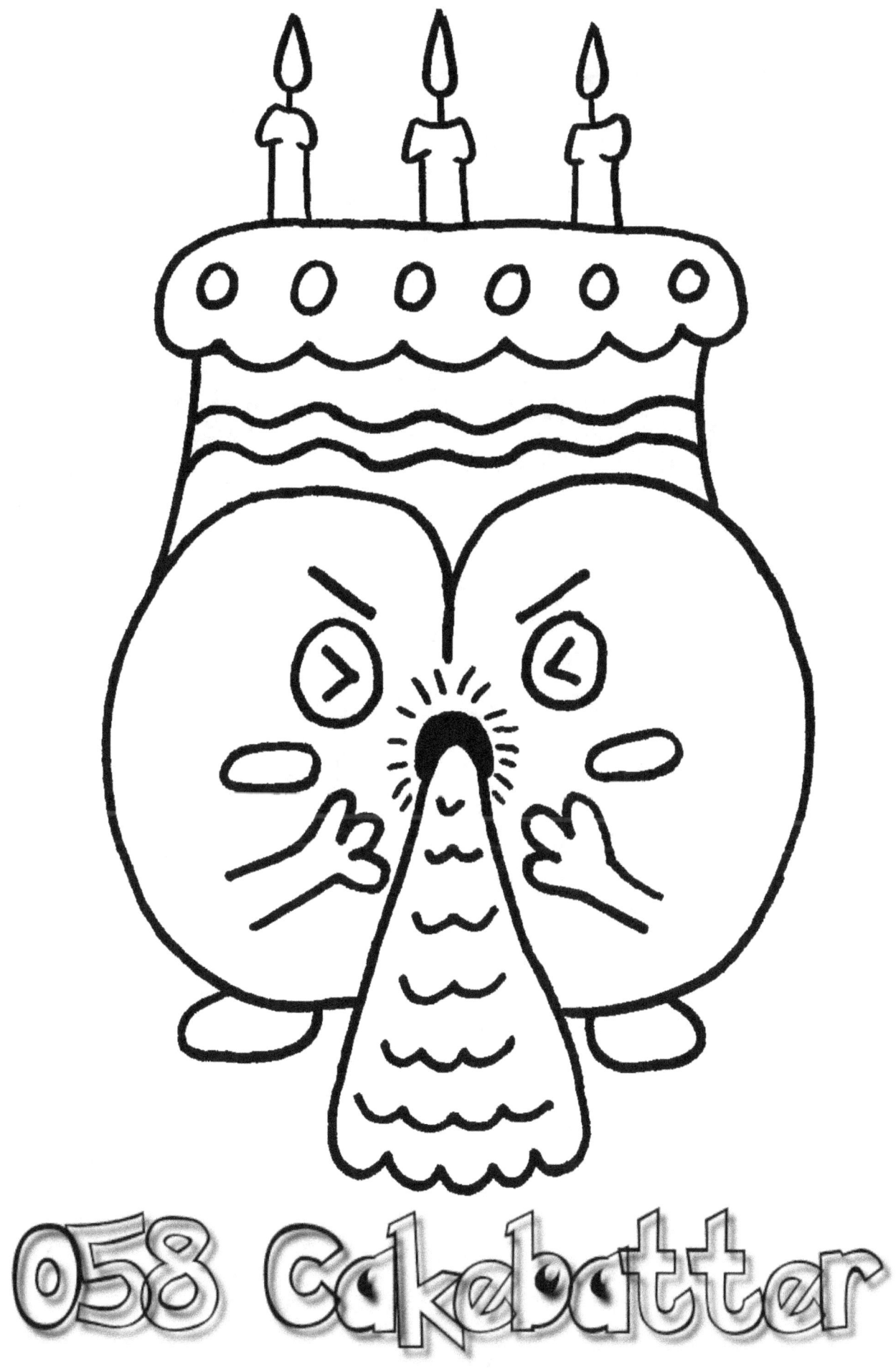

058 Cakebatter

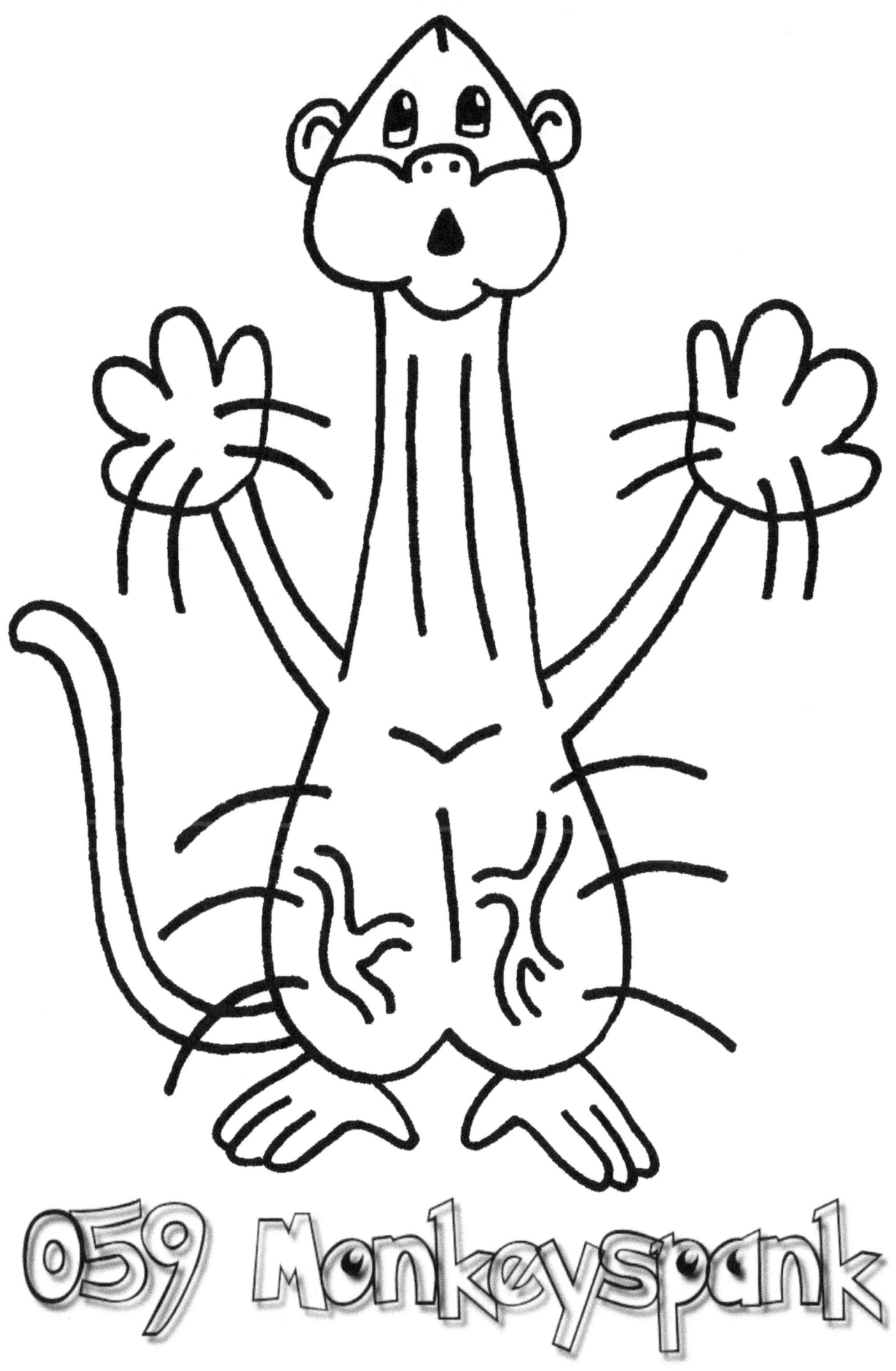

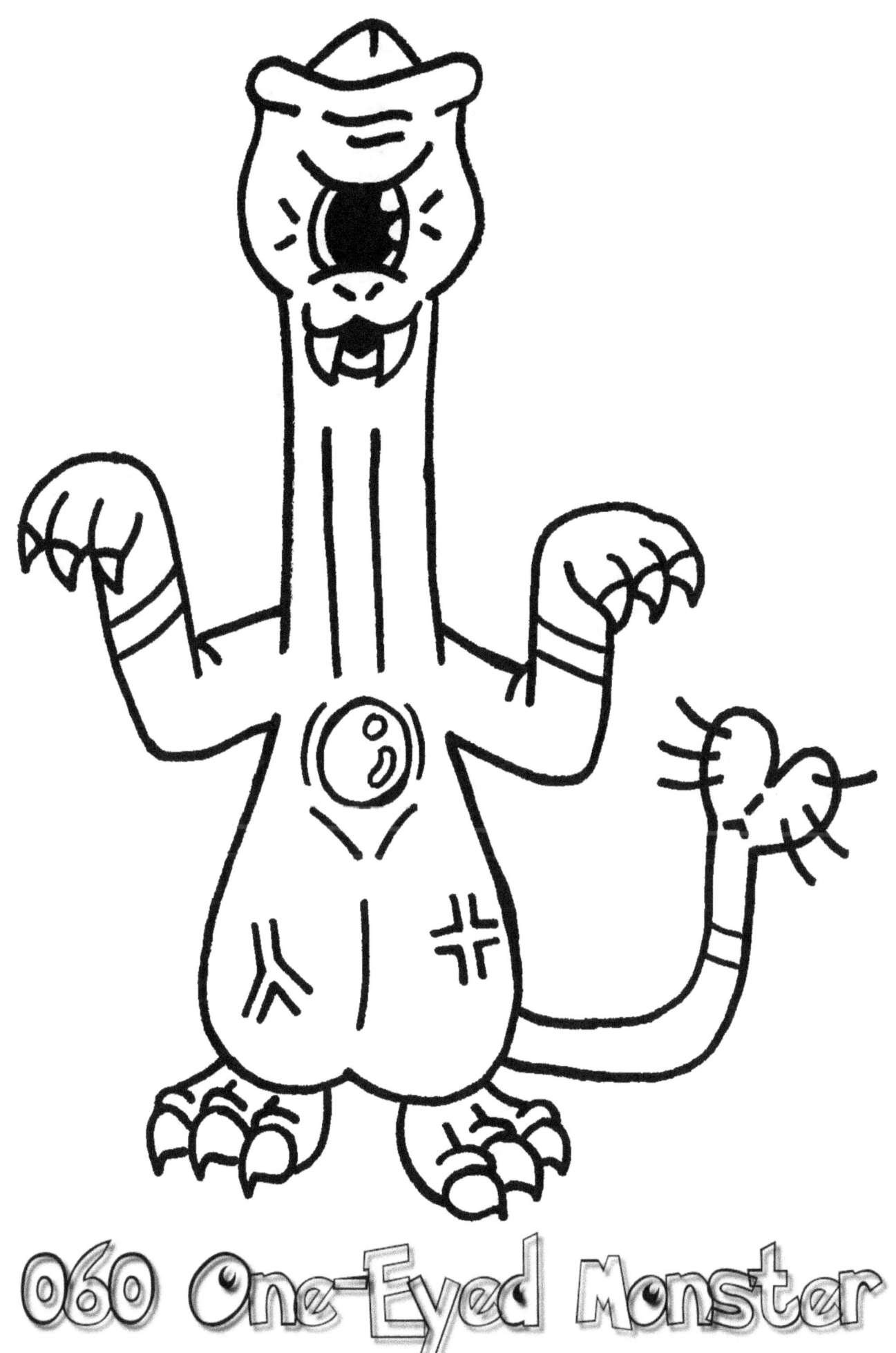

060 One-Eyed Monster

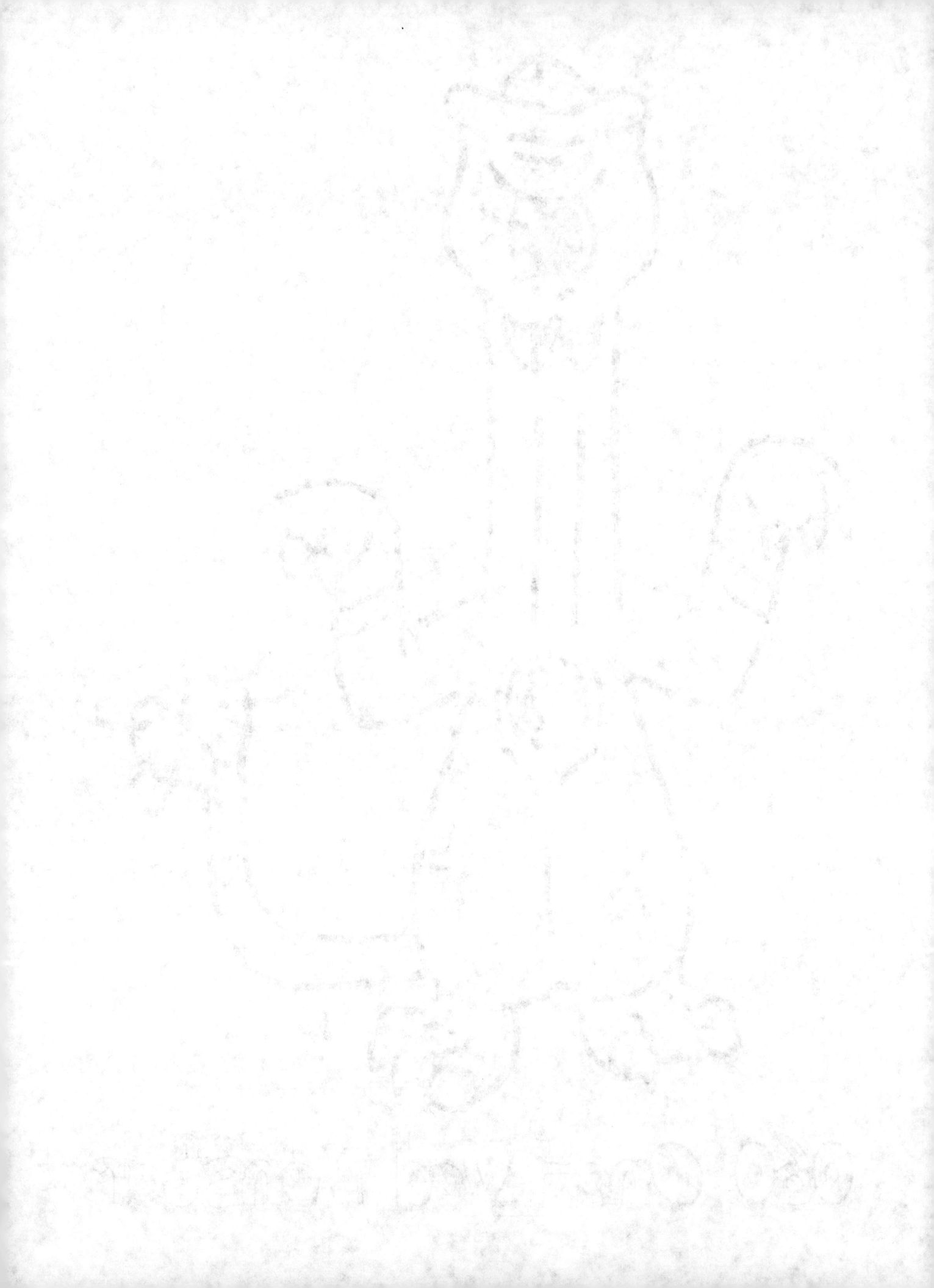

Thank you for your help cataloging all the Bukakkemon.

Share your finished coloring pages with me on social media!

Use #Bukakkemon and tag me.

On Twitter:
@AlexisHex

On Instagram:
@alexis.hex

Also find me on YouTube:
youtube.com/user/alexishex

Get a copy of the original outbreak:
Bukakkemon: An Adult Coloring Book Adventure!

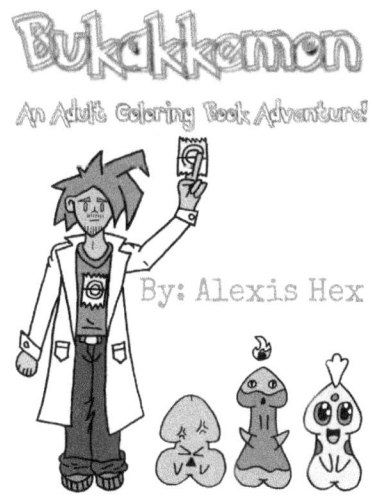

Available on Amazon

Until next time, Stay Hexy!